LIFE OF PI

Yann Martel

AUTHORED by Alice Cullina
UPDATED AND REVISED by Damien Chazelle

COVER DESIGN by Table XI Partners LLC
COVER PHOTO by Olivia Verma and © 2005 GradeSaver, LLC

BOOK DESIGN by Table XI Partners LLC

Published by GradeSaver LLC, www.gradesaver.com

First published in the United States of America by GradeSaver LLC. 2008

ISBN 978-1-60259-161-5

Printed in the United States of America

For other products and additional information please visit
http://www.gradesaver.com

Table of Contents

Biography of Martel, Yann (1963-)........1

About Life of Pi........3

Character List........5

Major Themes........9

Glossary of Terms........13

Short Summary........19

Quotes and Analysis........21

Summary and Analysis of Part 1, Chapters 1-11........25
Summary........25

Summary and Analysis of Part 1, Chapters 12-28........29
Summary........29

Summary and Analysis of Part 1, Chapters 29-36, and Part 2, Chapters 37-41........33
Summary........33

Summary and Analysis of Part 2, Chapters 42-56........35
Summary........35

Summary and Analysis of Part 2, Chapters 57-72........39
Summary........39

Summary and Analysis of Part 2, Chapters 73-85........43
Summary........43

Summary and Analysis of Part 2, Chapters 86-91........45
Summary........45

Summary and Analysis of Part 2, Chapters 92-94........47
Summary........47

Summary and Analysis of Part 3........49
Summary........49

Table of Contents

Suggested Essay Questions....51

Survival at Sea....55

Author of ClassicNote and Sources....57

Essay: Living a Lie: Yann Martel's Pi and his Dissociation from Reality....59

Quiz 1....63

Quiz 1 Answer Key....69

Quiz 2....71

Quiz 2 Answer Key....77

Quiz 3....79

Quiz 3 Answer Key....85

Quiz 4....87

Quiz 4 Answer Key....93

Biography of Martel, Yann (1963-)

Yann Martel was born on June 25, 1963, in Salamanca, Spain, to Emile and Nicole Martel, but spent his childhood living in a variety of different countries, including Costa Rica, France, India, Iran, Mexico, Turkey, Canada, and the United States. His parents, civil servants, were of French-Canadian descent, and their family eventually settled in Montreal.

Martel attended Trent University from 1981 to 1984, but graduated from Concordia University with a BA in philosophy in 1985. After graduating, along with writing and considering a career in politics or anthropology, he worked many different odd jobs—librarian, tree planter, dishwasher, security guard, and parking lot attendant. At the age of 27, he committed himself to writing.

Martel published his first work, *The Facts Behind the Helsinki Roccamatios and Other Stories*, a collection of four short stories, in 1993. It received warm critical reception, although it did not sell well. His first novel, *Self*, was published three years later, to more mixed reviews, and to similarly small sales. It is a fictional autobiography of the first thirty years of the narrator's life and involves two spontaneous gender changes.

After these two disappointments, Martel traveled to India to work on a third novel and figure out where his life was headed. He quickly realized the novel he was working on was going nowhere - but then he remembered something he had read about years before, and the idea for *Life of Pi* came to him.

Life of Pi was published in 2001 to warm, although somewhat mixed, critical reception, and, along with winning the Man Booker Prize, became an international best-seller. Many critics praised the book's ability to suspend disbelief even as it tells an amazingly fantastical tale. Those that had problems with the book most often referred to what they saw as Martel's heavy-handedness with the issue of belief in God, which they considered to underestimate both literature and religion. Other critics, however, praised Martel's handling of the potentially controversial religious material.

At the height of the book's popularity, there was a short-lived scandal involving an accusation of plagiarism. Martel has acknowledged that he thought of the premise after reading a review of the English translation of Moacyr Scliar's *Max and the Cats*; the Brazilian press accused Martel of cribbing that book. The similarities between the books, however, are few, and nothing came of the charges.

Martel is currently based in Montreal, although he frequently lives internationally. In 2002 and 2003, Martel worked as a professor in the Department of Comparative Literature at the Free University of Berlin, Germany.

About Life of Pi

Life of Pi began with some casual reading. Yann Martel was perusing through John Updike's rather negative review of *Max and the Cats*, a story about a Jewish family who run a zoo in Germany during the years leading up to the Holocaust. They decide to leave Germany, but the boat they take sinks, and only one member of the family survives, ending up on a lifeboat with a black panther.

Martel describes loving that premise, and being disappointed that he had not had the opportunity to do it better than the author. Years later, while in India, without a story he believed in or much hope, he suddenly remembered this premise, and the rest of *Life of Pi* came to him. For the next two years, in India and Canada, he researched the essentials—zoology, religion, survival at sea—and wrote what became an internationally best-selling novel.

Life of Pi was published in 2001, Yann Martel's third published work of fiction, and the one upon which most of his reputation is built. It was awarded Canada's 2001 Hugh MacLennan Prize for Fiction, in 2002, England's prestigious Man Booker Prize, and in 2003, South Africa's Boeke Prize. Critical reception was largely positive, focusing on Martel's ability to make a fantastical story at least plausible.

Some critics, however, found the theological preoccupations in the novel heavy-handed, unnecessary, inconsistent, or overly simplistic, while others thought that he successfully and deftly dealt with a potentially controversial subject, and admired his courage in writing an explicitly religious book in a predominantly secular country.

Because of Martel's acknowledged debt to Moacyr Scliar's *Max and the Cats*, there was a brief scandal at the height of *Life of Pi*'s popularity. The Brazilian press accused Martel of cribbing *Max and the Cats*, but the similarities between the two books were slight, and so the charges came to nothing.

Character List

Piscine Molitor Patel

Piscine is the narrator and protagonist, known as Pi. He is a small, slim man, with dark hair and eyes and an expressive face. He grew up in Pondicherry, but in his teens left for Canada with his family. He is deeply interested in religions, and considers himself a Hindu, Christian, and Muslim. At the University of Toronto he double-majors in Zoology and Religion.

Richard Parker

Richard Parker is a three-year-old Bengal tiger who is Pi's only companion at sea. He was captured as a cub with his mother, and ended up in the Pondicherry Zoo before it, and he, were sold.

The Author

The author is unnamed in the text, but throughout he includes descriptions of his interviews with Pi, and Pi as he is now in Canada.

Santosh Patel

Santosh is Pi's father. He ran a large hotel in Madras, before moving to Pondicherry to found and direct the Pondicherry Zoo. He has an intuitive understanding of his animals, and a great respect for them. He considers himself a modern, secular businessman, and so is surprised by Pi's religious pursuits. He dies in the sinking of the *Tsimtsum.*

Gita Patel

Gita is Pi's mother, a normally calm and unruffled woman. She, like Pi, is a big reader, but unlike Pi takes no interest in religion. She dies in the sinking of the *Tsimtsum.*

Ravi Patel

Ravi is Pi's older brother. He is very different from Pi--popular, a talented athlete in all the right sports (he is captain of the cricket team), and a merciless teaser. He dies in the sinking of the *Tsimtsum.*

The Frenchman

The Frenchman is another castaway, who meets Pi while rowing while they are both suffering from blindness. The Frenchman has decidedly carnivorous taste, and he tries to kill and eat Pi. He steps into Richard Parker's territory, however, and so is killed.

Orange Juice

Orange Juice is an orangutan who survives the shipwreck to end up in the lifeboat with Pi. She is forlorn over the loss of her beloved son. She dies fairly early on in a fight with the hyena.

Satish Kumar (teacher)

Satish is Pi's biology teacher at Petit Seminarie, an active Communist, and a weird-looking man with a bald and pointy head. He is Pi's favorite teacher, and the first avowed atheist that Pi ever meets. A great fan of the zoo, he sees it as his temple.

Father Martin

Father Martin is the kind priest who Pi meets in Munnar. He serves as Pi's introduction to Christianity, telling him the story of Christ's death on the cross and explaining that it was all inspired by love.

Satish Kumar (baker)

Satish Kumar is a Muslim mystic and baker, with the same name as Pi's favorite biology teacher. Satish the baker teaches Pi about Islam. He is poor, but very kind and generous. He is so plain-looking that Pi does not always recognize him.

Francis Adirubasamy

Francis is one of Pi's father's earliest business contacts, who became a good friend of the family. Pi calls him Mamaji. He is a former champion swimmer whose love for the sport never dies. He tries to teach this love of swimming to Pi's parents and Ravi, but Pi is the only one who he ever convinces. Francis is the one who introduces the author to Pi's story.

Auntie Rohini

Auntie Rohini is an older sister of Pi's mother. She is of a more traditional mind than Gita Patel, and is the first to take Pi to a Hindu temple as a small baby.

Tomohiro Okamoto

Mr. Okamoto is a member of the Maritime Department in the Japanese Ministry of Transport. He goes to Mexico to interview Pi in hopes of discovering what happened to the *Tsimtsum*.

Asuro Chiba

Mr. Chiba is Tomohiro Okamoto's junior colleague at the Maritime Department in the Japanese Ministry of Transport. He accompanies Mr. Okamoto to Mexico to interview Pi.

Meena Patel

Meena is Pi's wife. She works as a pharmacist and is a second generation Canadian.

Nikhil Patel

Nikhil is Pi's son. He plays baseball.

Usha Patel

Usha is Pi's four-year-old daughter.

Auntieji

Auntieji is Pi's foster mother in Toronto. She is a Quebecoise.

Sitaram

Sitaram is Pi's favorite zookeeper. He is in charge of the orangutans.

Major Themes

Belief in God

Belief in God is clearly a major theme in *Life of Pi*, and has been the most controversial in reviews of the book. Throughout the novel, Pi makes his belief in and love of God clear—it is a love profound enough that he can transcend the classical divisions of religion, and worship as a Hindu, Muslim, and Christian. Pi, although amazed by the possibility of lacking this belief, still respects the atheist, because he sees him as a kind of believer. Pi's vision of an atheist on his death bed makes it clear that he assumes the atheist's form of belief is one in God, without his realizing it until the end. It is the agnostic that truly bothers Pi; the *decision* to doubt, to lack belief in anything, is to him inexcusable. This is underscored in that essential passage in the novel when Pi asks the Japanese officials which of his two stories they preferred—he sees no reason why they should not believe the better story.

Pi's devotion to God is a prominent part of the novel; it becomes, however, much less prominent during his time aboard the lifeboat, when his physical needs come to dominate his spiritual ones. Pi never seems to doubt his belief in God while enduring his hardships, but he certainly focuses on it less. This in turn underscores the theme of the primacy of survival.

The Primacy of Survival

The primacy of survival is the definitive theme in the heart of the book, Pi's time at sea. This theme is clear throughout his ordeal—he must eat meat, he must take life, two things which had always been anathema to him before his survival was at stake. Survival almost always trumps morality, even for a character like Pi, who is deeply principled and religious. When Pi tells the second version of his story to the Japanese men, this theme is highlighted even more vividly, because he parallels his survival instincts in the second story to Richard Parker in the first—it is he, when he must survive, who steals food, he who kills the Frenchman. If the first version of the story is seen as a fictionalized version of the second, the very fact that he divides himself from his brutal survival instinct shows the power of that instinct.

Storytelling

The act of storytelling and narration is a significant theme throughout *Life of Pi*, but particularly in the narrative frame. That Pi's story is just that—a story—is emphasized throughout, with interjections from the author, Pi's own references to it, and the complete retelling of the story for the Japanese officials. (This is not to mention chapter ninety-seven, which contains two words: "The story.") By including a semi-fictional "Author's Note," Martel draws the reader's attention to the fact that not only within the novel is Pi's tale of survival at sea an unverified story, but the entire novel itself, and even the author's note, usually trustworthy, is a work of fiction.

This is not to say that Martel intends the reader to read *Life of Pi* through a lens of disbelief or uncertainty; rather, he emphasizes the nature of the book as a story to show that one can choose to believe in it anyway, just as one can choose to believe in God—because it is preferable to not believing, it is "the better story."

The Definition of Freedom

The true definition of freedom becomes a question early in *Life of Pi*, when Pi refutes the claims of people who think that zoos are cruel for restricting animals' freedom. Pi offers evidence against this, questioning the very definition of freedom. An animal in the wild is "free" according to the opponents of zoos, and it is true that that animal is not restricted in its movement by a physical cage. It is, however, profoundly restricted by its survival needs and its instincts. If that animal is guided solely by its need for food, water, and shelter, is it really free? If it will never intentionally wander outside of the territory it has defined for itself, is it really free? In a zoo, where the animal's needs are always provided, isn't it more free?

The question of freedom arises again as Pi finds himself in a fight for survival at sea. He is without responsibility to anyone else, he is without any need to be anywhere in the world, he is perpetually in motion; yet he has probably never been less free, for he must always be putting his survival above all else. An example of this is that he can no longer choose to be a vegetarian—he must eat meat to stay alive. Throughout *Life of Pi*, the primacy of survival, of life, greatly restricts "freedom," and thus redefines the very word.

The Relativity of Truth

The relativity of truth is not highlighted as a major theme in *Life of Pi* until the last part of the novel, when Pi retells the entire story to make it more plausible to the officials who are questioning him. He then asks the officials which story they liked better, since neither can be proven and neither affects the information they are searching for—how the ship sunk. This question implies that truth is not absolute; the officials can choose to believe whichever story they prefer, and that version *becomes* truth. Pi argues to the Japanese officials that there is invention in all "truths" and "facts," because everyone is observing everything from their own perspective. There *is* no absolute truth.

Science and Religion

The theme of science and religion as not opposed but in concert with each other is present primarily in the framing of the narrative. It is exemplified in Pi's dual major at the University of Toronto of Religion and Zoology, which he admits he sometimes gets mixed up, seeing the sloth that he studied as a reminder of God's miracles. Similarly, Pi's favorite teacher, Mr. Kumar, sees the zoo as the temple of his atheism. The theme of the connection between science and religion also is related to Pi's respect for atheists, because he sees that they worship science as he worships God, which he believes is not so very different.

Loss of Innocence

The theme of loss of innocence in *Life of Pi* is closely related to the theme of the primacy of survival. Its significance is reflected in the geographic structure of the book—in Part 1, Pi is in Pondicherry, and there he is innocent. In Part 2, Pi is in the Pacific Ocean, and it is there that he loses his innocence. That Part 2 begins, not chronologically with the *Tsimtsum* sinking, but with Pi inviting Richard Parker onto the lifeboat, also reflects this, for it represents Pi reaching out for what Richard Parker symbolizes—his own survival instinct. And it is this survival instinct that is at the heart of Pi's loss of innocence; it is this survival instinct that drives him to act in ways he never thought he could.

Throughout Part 2 there are other representative moments of a loss of innocence, besides the symbolic one of bringing Richard Parker onto the lifeboat. The most important of these is the death of the Frenchman, which Pi describes as killing a part of him which has never come back to life. That part can certainly be read as his innocence.

Glossary of Terms

acuity
keenness of hearing, sight, or intellect

agnostics
those who believe that the truth of religious or spiritual claims are impossible to prove or disprove

amenable
willing to cooperate; responsive to suggestion

anemic
suffering from a lack of hemoglobin in the blood, usually caused by a deficiency in iron

anthropomorphized
when nonhuman things have been treated or considered as human-like

arboreal
relating to trees

archipelago
a group or chain of islands

arduous
difficult and demanding

artesian well
a pumpless well that allows water to rise to the surface that has traveled through porous rock from a higher elevation

ashram
a community formed primarily for the spiritual uplifting of its members

attrition
slow destruction through wear and tear, weakening by persistent attack

brackish
salty

bracts

the plant parts from which the flowers grow

buoyant

able to float

cantankerous

easily angered and difficult to get along with

carapace

shell

carrion

the rotting flesh of a dead animal

cataleptic

in a state resembling a trance or unconsciousness, often associated with schizophrenia, epilepsy, or drug use

catholicity

wideness of range and inclusiveness, as in taste

chimera

a wildly unrealistic idea or hope

chromatic

relating to color

commensal

describing a relationship between two species in which one derives benefit from the association while the other is unharmed but also not benefited

cordate

heart-shaped

cosmogony

a theory of the creation of the universe

craw

throat or gullet

deputation

a group of people chosen to represent a larger group and act on their behalf

discordant
consisting of sounds that are clashing or harsh

dissembling
the adoption of a false appearance or pretending in order to conceal facts, feelings, or intentions

diurnal
active in daytime

durian
a foul-smelling but deliciously flavored fruit

feral
animals that live in the wild after having been domestically reared

ferment
an opening between two organs caused by disease or injury

founders
sinks or crumples

frugivorous
feeding primarily on fruit

gaff
a hooked fish pole, or to catch and hold with a hooked fish pole

garden of Gethsemane
believed to be the place where Jesus and the disciples prayed the night before Jesus' crucifixion

heijira
the emigration of Muhammad and his followers to Medina in 622CE

herald
something that gives an indication of something that is going to happen; a sign

in situ
in place

incongruously
unsuitably or inconsistently

ineluctably
inescapably

insouciant
having lighthearted unconcern; nonchalant

Kathakali dancer
a dancer in a highly stylized classical form of Indian dance-drama

kinetic
relating to motion

Kumkum powder
a powder used for social and religious markings in Hinduism

lampoonery
the ridicule or satirizing of someone or something

lasciviousness
lewdness

licit
allowed by law

lithesome
flexible; easily bendable

maharaja
a Hindu ruler

mange
an infectious skin disease of animals and sometimes humans

marauder
one who raids for plunder

memento mori
a work of art that is designed to remind the viewer of their imminent death, and the

general brevity and fragility of human life

menagerie
a collection of animals, usually for royalty

mien
general air or bearing

nadaswaram
a wind instrument that is highly popular in South India

oestrous
in heat

olfactory
relating to the sense of smell

onanists
those who practice masturbation

ordnance
military weapons and supplies

pandit
a scholar killed in Sanskrit and Hindu law, religion, music, or philosophy

porosity
the porous nature of something

prusten
the quietest tiger call, a puff through the nose used to express friendliness and harmless intentions

raiments
clothing

rambutan
a medium-sized tropical tree

rufous
of a reddish-brown color

ruminants
hoofed animals that chew cud

sambar
a dish common in South Indian and Sri Lankan communities

sanguinary
bloodthirsty

scimitars
an Arab or Turkish sword with a curved blade

ungulates
hoofed mammals

unpalatably
unpleasantly, in terms of taste

vagaries
unpredictable changes

venerable
worthy of respect; revered

virulent
extremely infectious or damaging

viscera
internal organs

wallah
one who sells or peddles something

Short Summary

Life of Pi tells the fantastical story of Pi Patel, a sixteen-year-old South Indian boy who survives at sea with a tiger for 227 days. Pi, born Piscine Molitor Patel, grows up in the South Indian city of Pondicherry, where his father runs the zoo. A precocious and intelligent boy, by the age of fifteen Pi—Hindu from an early age—has also adopted Christianity and Islam, and considers himself a pious devotee to all three religions.

Thanks to government upheaval that has long been distressing Pi's father, the Patels decide to close the Pondicherry Zoo and move to Canada when Pi is sixteen. Pi, his mother, father, and brother Ravi all board the *Tsimtsum* along with the zoo's animal inhabitants (who are on their way to be sold around the world).

An unexplained event causes the *Tsimtsum* to sink, and Pi is the only human to make it onto the lifeboat and survive. Along with Pi, the lifeboat contains a hyena, a zebra, Orange Juice the orangutan, and Richard Parker the tiger. The hyena kills and devours both the zebra and Orange Juice, before Richard Parker kills the hyena. Pi is left alone on a lifeboat with an adult male tiger.

There is no land in sight and the ocean is shark-infested, so Pi builds a raft which he attaches to the lifeboat, to keep himself at a safer distance from Richard Parker. Eventually, however, life on the raft proves too exhausting, and Pi realizes that if Richard Parker gets hungry enough, he will swim to it and kill Pi. So Pi decides that he must tame Richard Parker. Using a whistle, seasickness, and a turtle-shell shield, Pi manages to assert his authority over Richard Parker and delineate his own territory on the lifeboat, where he is comparatively safe from the tiger.

While at sea, Pi and Richard Parker face many challenges, traumas, tragedies, and miraculous occurrences. They never have sufficient food and fresh water, and the constant exposure is highly painful. A severe storm, which they miraculously survive, destroys the raft. Pi manages to capture and kill a bird. They are almost crushed by an oil tanker, which then passes by without seeing them.

During an especially severe period of starvation, Pi and Richard Parker both go blind. While blind, Pi hears a voice, and realizes that they have drawn near another lifeboat that contains a similarly starving and blind Frenchman. Pi and this man converse for a while, and bring their boats together. The Frenchman climbs onto Pi's boat, and immediately attacks him, planning to kill and eat him. He doesn't realize that there is a tiger on the boat, however, and accidentally steps into Richard Parker's territory. The tiger immediately attacks and kills him. Pi, saved at the cost of his attacker's life, describes this as the beginning of his true moral suffering.

Pi and Richard Parker come upon a weird island that is made of algae with trees protruding from it, teeming with meerkats but no other life. Pi and Richard Parker stay on the island for weeks, eating the algae and the meerkats, growing stronger, and bathing in and drinking from the fresh water ponds. They never stay on the island at night, however, Pi because he feels safer from the tiger in his delineated territory, and Richard Parker for a reason unknown to Pi. Pi eventually starts to sleep on the island, and while doing so realizes that the island is carnivorous—it emits acid at night that dissolves anything on its surface. Greatly disturbed by this, Pi takes Richard Parker, and they leave the island.

Pi and Richard Parker eventually land on the Mexican beach. Richard Parker immediately runs off into the jungle without acknowledging Pi, which Pi finds deeply hurtful. Pi is found, fed, bathed, and taken to a hospital. There, two Japanese men come to question Pi about what caused the *Tsimtsum* to sink. He tells his story, which they do not believe, so he offers them a more plausible version, with the animal characters replaced by other humans, which casts doubt on the original story.

Throughout the novel, the story is interrupted by the author's notes on Pi as he is now, telling this story to the author. After recovering in Mexico he went to Canada, where he spent a year finishing high school and then studied Religion and Zoology at the University of Toronto. At some point, he got married, and he now has two children. He still thinks of Richard Parker, and is still hurt by his final desertion.

Quotes and Analysis

"'So tell me, since it makes no factual difference to you and you can't prove the question either way, which story do you prefer? Which is the better story, the story with animals or the story without animals?' Mr. Okamoto: 'That's an interesting question?' Mr. Chiba: 'The story with animals.' Mr. Okamoto: 'Yes. The story with animals is the better story.' Pi Patel: 'Thank you. And so it goes with God.'"

Chapter 99, page 317

This quote is essential to the story-Yann Martel himself has described 'the better story' as the novel's key words. Here Pi enlarges the themes of truth, and story versus reality to encompass God, and all of life. If there is no way to prove that God's existence is true or untrue, and if the assumption of the truth either way in no way makes a factual difference, then why not choose to believe what Pi believes to be "the better story"-that God exists? This passage thus connects these central themes in the book, and so weaves everything together.

This passage contains several of the important themes and motifs of the novel. The final question, posed to the author, calls attention both to the fact that this story is being told through an intermediary, and to the arbitrariness of the telling-the book does indeed have a hundred chapters, and it would seem that the reason was a simple challenge from Pi. Similarly, Pi's injunction that "we must give things a meaningful shape" connects two of the novel's prominent themes, storytelling and belief in God. He believes that the act of storytelling, of giving things shape, can apply in life too, and thus one can shape one's own story in the most beautiful way by believing in God.

Chapter 94, page 285

This passage contains several of the important themes and motifs of the novel. The final question, posed to the author, calls attention both to the fact that this story is being told through an intermediary, and to the arbitrariness of the telling?the book does indeed have a hundred chapters, and it would seem that the reason was a simple challenge from Pi. Similarly, Pi?s injunction that ?we must give things a meaningful shape? connects two of the novel?s prominent themes, storytelling and belief in God. He believes that the act of storytelling, of giving things shape, can apply in life too, and thus one can shape one's own story in the most beautiful way by believing in God.

"This was the terrible cost of Richard Parker. He gave me a life, my own, but at the expense of taking one. He ripped the flesh off the man's frame and cracked his bones. The smell of blood filled my nose. Something in me died then that has never come back to life."

Chapter 90, page 255

This passage shows Pi in one of his darkest moments. The relatively shorter sentences here seem to imply a closing off. Pi can only bear to remember so much; he can list the sensations but he does not delve into the awful event's effect on his psyche. This moment, more than any other in the text, seems to mark an absence of God; it is also the moment where Pi's life is most explicitly threatened. Pi's guilt here is more easily understandable in the second version of the story, where it is he who kills the Frenchman. Either way, if Richard Parker is seen as a symbol of the pure survival instinct, this is the one moment in the text where that instinct wins out completely over morality and control.

"I can well imagine an atheist's last words: 'White, white! L-L-Love! My God!'-and the deathbed leap of faith. Whereas the agnostic, if he stays true to his reasonable self, if he stays beholden to dry, yeastless factuality, might try to explain the warm light bathing him by saying, 'Possibly a f-f-failing oxygenation of the b-b-brain,' and, to the very end, lack imagination and miss the better story."

Chapter 22, page 64

Pi here, in a short chapter, elucidates his opinion on atheists and agnostics. He sees atheists as capable of belief in God, for they have always had faith, just faith in science, rather than in God-which Pi believes is not inherently incompatible. On the other hand, the agnostic's doubt is to him an active choice not to believe, not to have the 'better story.'

"Animals in the wild lead lives of compulsion and necessity within an unforgiving social hierarchy in an environment where the supply of fear is high and the supply of food low and where territory must constantly be defended and parasites forever endured. What is the meaning of freedom in such a context? Animals in the wild are, in practice, free neither in space nor in time, nor in their personal relations."

Chapter 4, page 16

This passage is at the core of Pi's philosophy on freedom. He does not define freedom by a lack of bars, but by the ability to exercise free will with one's time, space, and relations. Animals, and anyone whose survival is continually threatened, do not have this luxury. This passage also foreshadows Pi's own prolonged fight for survival, which restricts his freedom and brings him down to the level of animals in other ways as well.

In this passage Pi again draws a connection between his two majors, Zoology and Religion. In both fields, he sees the human tendency towards self-centeredness as dangerous. In religion it leads to a lack of faith in God; in zoology, it leads to a possibly fatal misunderstanding of dangerous animals, or to a cruel treatment of an essentially innocent animal. The two lessons that Pi refers to in this passage are that of his father feeding a goat to one of the tigers in the zoo, and that of Richard Parker killing the Frenchman. It is interesting, however, that Pi, in telling his story, focuses more on Richard Parker's betrayal of him by leaving him without saying goodbye. Here, it seems, Pi has himself anthropomorphized Richard Parker; he is hurt by Richard Parker because he sees a mirror in him. Thus Pi himself, although he has claimed to have learned this important lesson, has not truly done so.

Chapter 8, page 31

In this passage Pi again draws a connection between his two majors, Zoology and Religion. In both fields, he sees the human tendency towards self-centeredness as dangerous. In religion it leads to a lack of faith in God; in zoology, it leads to a possibly fatal misunderstanding of dangerous animals, or to a cruel treatment of an essentially innocent animal. The two lessons that Pi refers to in this passage are that of his father feeding a goat to one of the tigers in the zoo, and that of Richard Parker killing the Frenchman. It is interesting, however, that Pi, in telling his story, focuses more on Richard Parker's betrayal of him by leaving him without saying goodbye. Here, it seems, Pi has himself anthropomorphized Richard Parker; he is hurt by Richard Parker because he sees a mirror in him. Thus Pi himself, although he has claimed to have learned this important lesson, has not truly done so.

"As an aside, story of sole survivor, Mr. Piscine Molitor Patel, Indian citizen, is an astounding story of courage and endurance in the face of extraordinarily difficult and tragic circumstances. In the experience of this investigator, his story is unparalleled in the history of shipwrecks. Very few castaways can claim to have survived so long at sea as Mr. Patel, and none in the company of an adult Bengal tiger."

This passage is the last paragraph of Life of Pi. It is an appropriate ending, because it essentially represents Mr. Okamoto accepting Pi's first story, and by extension, accepting God. Pi presents Mr. Okamoto with the possibility of shaping life as one would like to, seeing it in its most beautiful form. While Mr. Okamoto believed Pi's second, more tragic and horrible story, he prefers the first, and so Pi tells him to believe that one. It is not clear what choice Mr. Okamoto makes, until this final paragraph, which shows him accepting the tiger story which he at first finds so hard to believe.

Summary and Analysis of Part 1, Chapters 1-11

Summary

Life of Pi opens with a fictional author's note, explaining the origins of the book. The author explains that while in India and floundering on the book he is trying to write, he travels to Pondicherry, where an elderly man, Mr. Adirubasamy, tells him he has a story for him that will make him believe in God. Adirubasamy tells the author about Pi, who the author manages to find in Canada, where Pi relates his story.

That story begins in Chapter 1. Pi describes his education at the University of Toronto, his double major in religion and zoology, and why he is so fascinated by the sloth, an incredibly indolent creature. He says that his great suffering has made all subsequent pains both more unbearable and more trifling. He loves Canada, although he misses India deeply.

In Chapter 2, the author intervenes as narrator, describing Pi telling his story. In Chapter 3 we learn Pi's full name, Piscine Molitor Patel, and how he got it: he was named for a great pool, called the Piscine Molitor, in which his father's business associate and close friend, Francis Adirubasamy, swam in while in Paris.

Pi's father was a hotel manager, but left the business because he wanted to start a zoo, which he did in Pondicherry. Pi defends the zoo and attacks the common understanding of animals in the wild as free, and animals in a zoo as "unfree", for freedom in the wild is a myth: animals are restricted by their survival needs and their instincts.

When Piscine is 12, one of his classmates starts calling him "Pissing," so when Piscine graduates to Petit Seminaire, he shortens his name to Pi. At Petit Seminaire Pi has a biology teacher, Mr. Kumar, who comes to the zoo often and talks to Pi about his atheism. He becomes one of Pi's favorite teachers.

Pi describes the danger man poses to the animals in a zoo- the bad things he feeds them, the way he harms, tortures and kills them. One day Pi's father takes him and Ravi to the big cat house and makes them promise to never touch or in any way go near a tiger. To make sure they understand the full danger, he makes them watch as the tiger kills and eats a goat. This is just the first of many similar lessons he gives to his sons regarding the dangerous animals in the zoo.

Pi explains that the key to the science of zookeeping is to get the animals used to the presence of humans by diminishing their flight distance—the minimum distance at which an animal wants to keep a perceived enemy.

Pi explains that, no matter what, there will always be animals who try to escape from zoos, even though generally animals do not wish for "freedom." The escape attempts are often because the offending animal's enclosure is unsuitable, or because something within its enclosure has frightened its Animals are always escaping *from* something, never *to*.

As an example, in 1933 a female black leopard who was being abused by her co-habitating leopard escaped from the Zurich Zoo and managed to evade capture and survive for ten weeks before she was shot.

Analysis

The opening section of *Life of Pi* introduces many of the major themes of the novel, while providing a frame for the core of the story. The importance of storytelling as a theme is immediately apparent, as the line between fiction and reality is blurred in the opening Author's Note, a semi-fictional, semi-true account of Yann Martel's writing of *Life of Pi*. The author's note also contains the claim that is at the heart of the novel—that this story will make you believe in God.

Whether or not the reader is, at the end, convinced of this, the characters are. The author/narrator, who never seems too skeptical, becomes a full-fledged believer. Mr. Okamoto and Mr. Chiba, who at first have little faith in Pi's tale, at the end accept it, and by extension, God. In the first section, however, the reader knows none of this, nor has any idea how the story to come will instill faith. Yet by presenting this as an option, and by focusing on the themes of storytelling and the connections between science and religion, the book's opening paves the way for the final leap of faith that the novel will ask of the reader.

Foreshadowing is used extensively. The reader does not know much of the fantastic story to come, nor who Richard Parker is, but it becomes clear that animals, survival, and freedom will all be important in the tale. Pi argues against the belief that zoo animals are unhappy because they are not free, explaining that freedom in the wild, where one must always fight to survive, is a myth. This assertion foreshadows Pi's own later loss of freedom while at sea, and the ways that the fight to survive diminish his humanity.

The danger of wild animals is also previewed here: Richard Parker, yet to be introduced, will embody this danger, whether in a literal or a symbolic sense. If literal, the knowledge Pi and the reader gain regarding the brutality of tigers will make Pi's journey and survival all the more miraculous. If symbolic, this section foreshadows how dangerous Pi himself will become as he loses his humanity in his fight to remain alive.

Finally, this section discusses rather extensively the connections between religion and science. Pi cannot keep his dual majors, religion and zoology, straight, although to the typical person they would seem fairly disparate. His favorite teacher, Mr.

Kumar, sees the zoo as his temple. And Pi compares the misconceptions involved in zoos, and freedom, as similar to the misconceptions many have about religion. In this way, Pi opens the reader to the idea that belief in anything can be belief in God.

Summary and Analysis of Part 1, Chapters 12-28

Summary

The author mentions that Pi sometimes gets agitated by his own story, and that the author is tortured by the spiciness of the food Pi makes for him.

Pi explains that an animal will attack you for entering its enclosure only because you have threatened its territory, and that most hostile behavior is the expression of social insecurity. The socially inferior animals will make the greatest effort to befriend the alpha-human, be he the lion tamer or the zookeeper, because they have the most to gain from his friendship and his protection from the other animals.

The author describes Pi's house, which is filled with religious symbols and idols and articles of devotion-but of many different religions, not just one. Pi describes the time when his Auntie Rohini takes him, as an infant, on his first trip to a temple, thereby beginning his religious life. Pi then describes what it is that makes him a Hindu, and why he has been a Hindu his whole life, but why that does not have to mean he is closed off from ideas outside of Hinduism, and why all religions are connected.

When he is fourteen, Pi and his family go on a trip to Munnar. While exploring the place, Pi comes upon a Christian church. He watches the priest, then returns to the church the next day and has tea with Father Martin. Father Martin explains the story of Christ and his death, but Pi finds the tale irritating: he cannot believe it.

He meets with Father Martin for three days straight, continuing to ask questions. On his last day in Munnar, Pi tells Father Martin that he wants to be a Christian, and Father Martin tells him that he already is, for he has met Christ in good faith.

When he is fifteen, Pi comes upon the Muslim section of Pondicherry while exploring his neighborhood. He ends up in a small bakery, and while he is talking to the baker, the call to prayer comes and Pi watches the baker pray. He finds the physicality of it satisfying.

Pi returns to see the baker and asks him about Islam, which he finds beautiful. The baker, named Satish Kumar, allows Pi to explore this faith, and Pi recounts two experiences during which he encounters God.

The author considers what Pi has said about religion in an aside, and then Pi imagines an atheist and an agnostic on their respective deathbeds, which for him exemplifies why he can respect the first but not the second—one has belief where the other only has doubt.

Pi's parents find out that he is a practicing Hindu, Christian, and Muslim, when they run into his priest, imam and pandit at the same time. The three religious men, upon realizing that each has only a third of Pi, break into heated arguments over whose is the true religion. Pi says that he just wants to love God, which quiets the three of them effectively. Ravi then finds out about Pi's tri-piousness, and mocks him for it. Pi finds it harder to practice his religions as people react to his multiplicity of beliefs.

Pi asks his father for a prayer rug and to be baptized. His father tries to convince him to pick one religion, and tells him to talk to his mother, who tries to convince him of the same thing. He is unswayed. Pi overhears his parents discussing his religious fervor. They decide to just accept it, and wait for it to pass: Pi gets his prayer rug and is baptized.

Analysis

This section deals primarily with one of Pi's central characteristics—his piousness. Pi here tells the story of how he became Hindu, Christian, and Muslim, and it becomes clear to the reader that God is central to Pi, and was even in his early years. That this kind of piousness is unique becomes equally evident when we see the three holy men in Pi's life fight with each other over whose religion is best. Even the men who have helped Pi to find God in so many different ways become divisive over details.

This section also illuminates Pi's devotion to his religions, for we see him up against many obstacles. The holy men themselves do not want to share him with other religions, his parents would prefer he were as secular as they were, and his brother mocks him. Even the religious communities see him differently once they know that he is not solely devoted to any one of their respective creeds. Yet none of this dims Pi's dedication to his three religions, and to God.

However, after this section, Pi's piousness is never again quite as central to the narrative, and during his suffering at sea, though he makes allusions to spirituality, his physical fight for survival dominates. Thus, his dedication to God here, which requires overcoming obstacles, only serves to emphasize the overpowering nature of his fight for survival later, as that fight seems to diminish his devotion to God.

This section also reiterates the theme of storytelling. In one chapter the author describes his own writing of the story, trying to remember Pi's exact words and the impression they left on him. The next chapter contains those words the author was trying to remember. He exists as a figure standing *between* the story and the reader; even if he remembers and tells it "perfectly", he is nonetheless controlling our perspective of it, and thus rendering the heretofore objective subjective.

It also becomes clear here - in Chapter 21 specifically - that the author is already beginning to open up to Pi's story, to find faith in Pi's words. Storytelling and belief in God are inextricably linked; both require faith. Moreover, within a story, one may find God.

Summary and Analysis of Part 1, Chapters 29-36, and Part 2, Chapters 37-41

Summary

In February 1976, the Tamil Nadu government is brought down by Mrs. Gandhi's government, an event that deeply worries Pi's father. Eventually, the stress of trying to keep his zoo profitable during a time of bad governance leads him to decide to move his family to Canada.

The author finds out for the first time that Pi is married, and meets his wife, Meena. He will also meet Pi's son, daughter, dog and cat, none of whom he at first knew existed.

Back to Pi's story: Mr. Kumar the baker asks Pi to visit the zoo, and Pi shows him around. While there, they run into Mr. Kumar the teacher. Together they each feed a carrot to a zebra. Pi describes instances of animals becoming companions across species.

The author describes Pi showing him photographs and memorabilia. There are very few pictures from Pi's life in India, and those he has were sent over by Mr. Adirubasamy, after the sinking of a ship called the *Tsimtsum*.

The Patels sell the zoo and all its animals, but it takes a year to complete the process of moving the animals. On June 21st, 1977, the Patels board the *Tsimtsum* and leave India.

Part 2 of *Life of Pi* begins with the sinking of the *Tsimtsum*. Prior to this catastrophe, Pi has enjoyed the trip immensely, tracking the boat's daily progress with gleeful precision. Then, four days out into the Pacific, some noise, possibly an explosion, wakes Pi in the middle of the night. Pi goes out to explore what the noise was. Out on the main deck Pi finds there is a severe storm, but, as that is nothing unusual for the journey, he is only excited. It doesn't take long, however, for him to notice that the ship is listing severely. He goes back inside and tries to get back to his family, but he finds flooding in his way. It becomes clear the ship is sinking, and what's more, the animals have somehow gotten loose. Pi finds some crew members, who put a life jacket on him and throw him overboard.

Pi lands in a partially lowered lifeboat. A zebra jumps in after him, which causes the boat to drop into the water.

Pi sees Richard Parker, the tiger, and helps him. At the last minute he realizes it is very stupid to share a lifeboat with a tiger, but it's too late: Richard Parker has already gotten on. Pi jumps off and grabs the lifebuoy. Just then, he sees a shark coming. He uses an oar to create a projection, and hangs between the water and the boat, the tiger and the sharks.

Pi watches the *Tsimtsum* sink, but sees no other signs of life. Eventually he must get further back into the lifeboat, where he finds the zebra is still alive but suffering from a broken leg. Pi wonders why Richard Parker has not killed it. Then he sees a hyena on the boat too, which he believes means that Richard Parker must have fallen off.

Analysis

This section contains the turning point of the novel, when Pi's life goes from fairly normal to tragic. At the end of Part 1, Pi's family has just begun what appears to be an exciting journey to a new country. Instead, Pi soon becomes an orphan, with everyone and everything he has ever known sunk into the ocean.

The end of Part 1 contains more clues for what will happen in Part 2. Pi helps his Muslim mentor and his favorite teacher - both named Mr. Kumar - feed a zebra together, who they view as a beautiful and noble creature. Here, in the zoo, that may be true, but in the next section, after the sinking, the zebra will suffer agonizing pain - and in the ugliest manner. The scene with the zebra in the zoo can thus be interpreted as symbolizing the last moment of Pi's innocence, before he too is made ugly by suffering.

Toward the end of Part 1, the author offers clues hinting that the crossing of the Pacific will serve as a profound loss of innocence and fundamental change for Pi. The author is shown pictures from Pi's life, but only ones after the crossing are clear; there are very few from before, and they tend not to show much.

The final line of Part 1 is also significant: "This story has a happy ending." It is a powerful sentence, because the reader has not yet learned of any of Pi's suffering; the need for such an ending is not as yet clear. Ironically, this declaration of hope and optimism spells doom, foreshadowing the devastating trials and tribulations Pi must soon encounter.

The beginning of Part 2 jumps around chronologically, but only within a small period of time. It in fact opens with Pi encouraging Richard Parker to enter the lifeboat. That, and not the ship's sinking, is in effect posited as the representative turning point. If we read Richard Parker as a symbol for Pi's survival instinct, it is interesting that Pi invites him to the lifeboat—it is an active choice, to survive, to become part beast. That he quickly regrets this decision, and realizes that it may imperil his spirit, is also significant.

Summary and Analysis of Part 2, Chapters 42-56

Summary

Pi finally sees another sign of life—Orange Juice, the orangutan, floating on a net filled with bananas. She steps into the boat, and Pi pulls the net aboard. The hyena runs in circles around the boat all morning. Pi remains tense the whole time, but eventually the hyena stops, vomits, and lies down.

There are flies everywhere, and night falls. Pi hears all kinds of noises that terrify him, but he makes it to the next morning. As the sun rises again, Pi regains hope. Then he notices that the hyena has ripped off the zebra's broken leg, and is eating it. Pi also notices that Orange Juice is very sea-sick. In the afternoon, a sea turtle appears.

As the sun starts to set again, Pi notices there are sharks circling. Orange Juice looks mournfully for her son, and the hyena attacks the zebra again, essentially eating her from the inside out. When the sun sets, Pi realizes that there is no longer any hope that his family is still alive.

The next morning, the zebra is somehow still alive, but by noon it finally dies. Tension rises between the hyena and Orange Juice, and the hyena attacks. Orange Juice defends herself impressively, but eventually the hyena kills her. When Pi prepares to fight the hyena to his own death, he sees that Richard Parker is still on the boat.

Pi tells the story of how Richard Parker got his name. He was captured as a cub with his mother, and the hunter who caught him intended to name him Thirsty. The paperwork got mixed up, however, and somehow the hunter's name wound up listed as Thirsty, while the tiger was given the hunter's name—Richard Parker.

Because Pi has now lost all hope, he paradoxically perks up—he has nothing left to lose. He realizes that he is dying of thirst, and, hoping to find fresh water on the boat, begins to explore. While investigating the boat, Pi finds fresh water, and after drinking two liters feels infinitely better. He then eats for the first time in three days.

Pi considers his options, and realizes he has no chance of survival either staying in the boat with Richard Parker, or leaving the boat and trying to swim to safety. He decides, however, that he is not going to give up and accept death. He builds a raft using oars, life jackets, and rope.

Right as Pi is about to finish, Richard Parker emerges, and swiftly kills the hyena. As the tiger then turns toward Pi, a rat suddenly appears and runs up Pi's body and to the top of his head. As Richard Parker hesitates to step onto the tarpaulin toward Pi, he throws the rat into his mouth and descends back under the tarpaulin, seemingly satisfied. Pi manages to finish the raft and throws it overboard; it floats, so he gets on it and, using a rope, keeps it about thirty feet from the boat.

During Pi's first night on the raft, it rains from dusk to dawn. While he is kept awake by the downpour, Pi considers possible plans to rid the boat of Richard Parker. He realizes that his best chance of survival is simply to wait for Richard Parker to die of starvation or dehydration, as Pi's own supplies are likely to last much longer.

In the morning the rain eventually clears and Pi gets some sleep. But upon waking he realizes how vast the sea is, how small his raft is, and it occurs to him that Richard Parker can both survive on saline water, and will likely swim to Pi's raft and kill him if he gets hungry enough. Stricken, Pi describes the utter power of fear.

Analysis

This section will by the end of the novel emerge as thematically very important: it contains the portion of the story paralleled in Pi's second telling, yet to come. In this first telling, the events—the deaths of the zebra, Orange Juice, and the hyena—are clearly traumatic, but not devastating. In Pi's second go-around, however, the moments of narrative are imbued with the horror of a 227-day ordeal—the cruel murder of a sailor, cannibalism, a mother's brutal murder, and Pi's choice to kill another man in retaliation and for survival.

The primary concern in this section is survival. From here until the end of the novel, survival will be Pi's, and the story's, driving force; here it is a new burden, and Pi learns for the first time how it will change him. It is not all bad—it allows Pi to be distracted from the tragic and awful loss of his whole family—but it is more all-consuming than he could have expected.

The motif of naming comes up again in this section, too, when we learn the origin of Richard Parker's unusual name. Throughout *Life of Pi*, Pi always refers to Richard Parker by name—he is never "the tiger." That this name is meant for a human adds to the feeling that Pi has humanized Richard Parker. He manages to survive with him for so long, but does, in the end, pay for it emotionally, because he expects a human-like goodbye from the tiger - a good-bye he does not receive.

This section also emphasizes Pi's profound isolation. The size of the ocean, the overwhelming power of nature as it rains down on him, make his odds of survival seem bleak, his situation dire. Pi does not accept this, however, and decides that he will survive. Yet, even in making this decision, he quickly realizes that the one plan he has come up with that seems at all plausible will not succeed.

The power of nature is also emphasized in terms of emotional toll. Pi loses all hope, accepts his parents' and brother's deaths, and feels true, overpowering fear. Yet he also finds freedom in his hopelessness, and he discovers that he has an ultimate will to survive that cannot be squelched.

Summary and Analysis of Part 2, Chapters 57-72

Summary

Richard Parker watches Pi contentedly after finishing his hyena meal. He then makes a sound Pi has heard *of* but never heard—"prusten", a puff through the nose used to express friendliness and harmless intentions. This leads Pi to realize that his only choice for survival is to tame Richard Parker. This is a relief to him, because he had realized his chances of outliving the tiger were very low, and somehow Richard Parker's presence kept him from thinking too much about his family and his hopelessness. Pi begins the training from his raft.

Pi reads over the boat's survival manual, then thinks over all the things he has to do with long-term survival in mind. He realizes that he can use the raft to change the orientation of the boat, leading it to rock more unpleasantly side to side. He also sees cockroaches, the last remnants of life on the boat besides Richard Parker, jump overboard. Pi uses the solar still to make fresh water from the sea water, then spends the day improving his raft. When he is finished, he looks down and realizes the sea is teeming with life, which he watches until the sun sets.

Pi wakes during the night, and realizes that his suffering is taking place in a grand setting, and accepts, temporarily, that it, and he, are insignificant in the grand scheme of things.

He decides to fish. He cuts up his remaining shoe to use as bait, but loses all of it to the fish, who avoid the hook. Pi goes onto the lifeboat to search for something else to use as bait, and a school of flying fish go by, many landing in the boat.

Pi gets one of these fish and takes it to the raft to use as bait, but he has a hard time killing it—he finally manages, but he weeps over it. It is successful as bait, however, and he manages to catch a three-foot dorado, which he has much less psychological trouble killing. He then gives it to Richard Parker.

Pi starts to worry about the water situation, as Richard Parker is showing signs of thirst. He checks the solar stills without much hope, but finds that they have indeed created a fair amount of salt-free water. He pours the water into a bucket and gives it to Richard Parker.

Pi reports that, all told, he survived 227 days at sea. He describes his average day, and how he managed to keep busy. He describes the salt water boils that he would get after his clothes fully disintegrated. He tried to learn about navigation from his survival handbook, but it assumed a basic knowledge that he did not have, and he did not have the strength to alter the boat's course much anyway.

Pi describes how his fishing ability improved as time passed. He started to use his cargo net as a lure, which attracted fish to his raft. He also realized it was easy to catch turtles, although not at all easy to haul them aboard. The underside of the raft became a small sea community, which Pi used for snacks and as something to watch to calm his nerves.

After time, Pi gets used to the motion of the sea and the wind, but he still cannot ever sleep well because of his anxiety. He gives up completely on being rescued by a ship, and just hopes for land.

The first time that Pi kills a sea turtle, it is because the survival manual recommends their blood for drinking. Richard Parker has started to tolerate Pi on the tarpaulin when it is hot out, but Pi is tired of having to fear him, and decides it is time to impose himself and carve out his own territory.

To do this, Pi intentionally provokes Richard Parker to step into Pi's territory, at which point he blows his whistle furiously and uses the raft to make the lifeboat go broadside - and thus rock uncomfortably for Richard Parker - so that the tiger will associate his nausea with the sound of the whistle. He allows Richard Parker to recover, then repeats the process until the whistle alone is enough to make the tiger retreat.

Analysis

This section paradoxically marks both the beginning of Pi's descent into more beast-like behavior, driven by survival needs to a greater degree than Pi would have believed himself capable of, and the beginning of Pi's control over Richard Parker, who represents the truly wild and bestial. Pi, a lifelong vegetarian, is here driven both to eat meat, and to willfully take life for the first time in his life.

He adjusts to this surprisingly quickly—the flying fish that he very reluctantly and very unhappily kills to use as bait catches him a dorado, which he almost gleefully beats to death. He eventually is even driven to kill a sea turtle, which he finds to be wonderful and one of his favorite foods.

As Pi grows more carnivorous, he comes to realize that he must tame Richard Parker. He begins the training that he has devised so that he can have his own territory on the lifeboat and feel relatively safe there. Although it is not easy and is highly dangerous, he eventually manages to mark out his own territory and exert a certain amount of dominance over Richard Parker.

It is within this section also that time loses meaning. Before this, even at sea, there has been some feeling of chronology in Pi's story. Within this section, however, Pi declares that he was at sea for 227 days, and with that the chronology stops. Pi, who can no longer keep track of time - which proves something of a blessing.

The danger of loneliness also rears its head. Pi's isolation is so extreme that he finds comfort in the sea-life communities that come to grow around his raft. Part of Pi's desire to train, rather than kill, Richard Parker comes from his deep loneliness—although Richard Parker is not much of a companion, he distracts Pi from his greater troubles, and in this takes on a great importance.

Summary and Analysis of Part 2, Chapters 73-85

Summary

Pi's training of Parker is only successful because Parker does not actually want to attack him: all animals know that the risks of physical violence are great, so they avoid it when possible, Pi notes.

Pi's greatest wish, above salvation, is for a book - but all he has is his survival manual and the diary he keeps for himself. He adapts his religious rituals to the circumstances, and does his best to fight the despair that so often comes. On what he estimates is his mother's birthday, Pi sings happy birthday to her.

Pi notices that Richard Parker tries to hide his feces, which is a sign of deference to Pi, so he makes a show of collecting the feces as a psychological ploy.

Pi's store of survival rations diminishes, and so he has to eat less and less. His mood grows more and more closely associated with how big a meal he has been able to have. One time he even goes so far as to try to eat Richard Parker's feces, but he can tell that there is nothing nutritious in it, so he spits it out.

The sharks are always around, but never do anything that really threatens Pi, and so he grows to like them. One day he manages to pull a smaller shark into the boat, where it gets into a battle with Richard Parker. After that Pi only goes for the baby sharks, which he kills by stabbing in the eye.

One day, while a school of flying fish is jumping over the boat, Pi manages to catch a dorado, and faces off with Richard Parker over it. Richard Parker eventually backs down, and Pi feels that his mastery of the tiger is complete.

It is not just Pi's use of seasickness that keeps Richard Parker from killing him, but the fact that Richard Parker is a zoo animal, and Pi was his source of fresh food and water most of the time.

Pi explains that the scarcity of fresh water is the largest problem throughout his entire journey. He also has to give most of his food to Richard Parker, so he learns to eat more indiscriminately and quickly.

One day comes a storm worse than any Pi has faced. Pi is forced to roll the tarpaulin down and get under it, and into Richard Parker's territory, to avoid drowning. The storm lasts all day and into the night, and when it finally ends Pi realizes that his raft is gone except for a piece or two. The boat also is damaged, and much of the food and supplies are lost. Luckily, one whistle remains.

Pi describes the whales that he sees, which always lift his spirits. He and Parker are also visited fairly regularly by dolphins, and very rarely by birds, one of which Pi manages to kill.

Analysis

In this section, we see Pi's continued descent toward the bestial. As the food becomes scarcer, he notices that his own eating has come to resemble Richard Parker's—fast, savage, indiscriminate. He also becomes more courageous in his choice of prey, going after baby sharks, and at one time even an adult shark.

This section also shows Pi achieving real dominance over Richard Parker. Richard Parker tries to hide his feces from Pi and backs down when Pi fights him for a dorado—all signs that, even as Pi is becoming more animal-like himself, he is dominating Richard Parker more fully. Thus, although it required intellect for Pi to tame Richard Parker, it seems the primal survival instinct in Pi - the *animal* in him - is more powerful and potentially more useful.

This section also stresses Pi's proximity to death. The storm is the primary example: Pi is saved by luck but left with only one whistle; that whistle in turn represents all that stands between life and death at the jaws of Richard Parker.

That said, Martel does dwell here on the more peaceful side of the animal kingdom as well. The whales, dolphins, and even sharks come to provide a kind of companionship for Pi. His description of these animals, however, further emphasizes how much his struggle for survival has altered him. Even when it comes to the peaceful dolphins and beautiful birds, Pi thinks of animals as, above all, possible food.

This seems to foreshadow what will come with the introduction of the Frenchman, when Pi descends so far as to eat human flesh. Of his animal companions, only Richard Parker is still safe from becoming Pi's food, because Pi would be incapable of killing him. But as animals that Pi would never have considered killing and eating in his past life become possible meals, the line between friend and food grows blurred, making the possibility of eating human flesh later less extreme.

Summary and Analysis of Part 2, Chapters 86-91

Summary

One day Pi sees an oil tanker coming toward him and Parker. All too quickly it is bearing down on them, and our hero only just misses getting crushed. Unfortunately, the tanker passes without ever seeing Pi, and his ordeal continues. Another day, Pi comes upon a large amount of floating garbage. He pulls an empty wine bottle from the refuse and places a message inside.

When he needs escape, Pi covers his face with a wet cloth, which asphyxiates him just enough to put him into a dream-like state.

Slowly, Pi and Richard Parker waste away as do all their supplies. They are losing weight and becoming more and more dehydrated. Excerpts from Pi's diary show more and more loss of hope, until he writes "I die" and his pen runs out of ink.

After one three-day span of not having anything to eat, Pi notices that Richard Parker has gone blind. Then his own eyes start to itch, and soon he cannot see anything. He becomes sure that both he and Richard Parker will die.

As he lays down and prepares for death, he hears a voice. He is sure it must be a hallucination, but he enters into conversation with it all the same. He and the voice discuss what they would eat if they could have anything, and Pi realizes that he is talking to Richard Parker.

He drifts out of consciousness, then hears a voice again, and returns to conversation. He realizes now that the voice is that of another man, a Frenchman, also blind, also in a lifeboat rowing beside him, also starving. Pi and the Frenchman manage to draw up next to each other, and the stranger climbs into Pi's boat. He immediately dives on Pi and tries to kill him, with the intention of eating him, but the Frenchman is attacked and killed by Richard Parker.

Pi explores the dead man's boat, and finds some food and water. As he manages to rehydrate, his vision slowly comes back. He finds the remains of the man still in the boat, and uses some of his flesh for fish bait. He goes so far as to eat some of it, but stops the minute he catches a fish again.

Analysis

This section represents a decisive turning point in Pi's narrative and arc. Here Pi truly loses his innocence, survival exacts the dearest cost, and his suffering becomes tangible. Ironically, this section also continues sparks of real hope. After all, Pi encounters not one but *two* boats - a miraculous stroke of good fortune that comes to naught.

The dashing of these hopes comes almost as soon as Pi can appreciate them. First, the oil tanker that could save him almost kills him, then continues on into the distance without ever seeing him. Second, and most horribly, Pi's first interaction with another human since the *Tsimtsum* sank brings not the companionship he is so excited for, but instead attempted murder and brutal death—and with it, profound guilt.

Pi makes it clear that whether the first story is taken symbolically or literally, the Frenchman's death is in either way caused by Pi's own fight for survival. Thus he must forever accept that his survival came at the cost of another's life. Whether Richard Parker, or the survival instinct that Richard Parker symbolizes, is the actual killer seems irrelevant to Pi, since the result is the same.

The despair and suffering that follow the Frenchman's death are highlighted by the excitement that precedes it, though that excitement is tinged with surrealism. Since Part 2 and Pi's loss of all human companionship, the novel has had little dialogue, understandably. So with the arrival of the Frenchman, who Pi and the reader both first assume to be some kind of hallucination, the novel's form suddenly changes course in dramatic fashion. This sudden proliferation of dialogue, combined with Pi's extremely weak state and blindness, and confused belief that he is speaking to Richard Parker, make this scene the least believable of Pi's tale. The scene's ending, however, makes it clear that this is also the scene that Pi would be least likely to make up—its horror would serve him no purpose. Here, then, we see one of the few instances in which Pi does not try to tell the better story: he cannot incorporate God into this awful memory.

Summary and Analysis of Part 2, Chapters 92-94

Summary

One day Pi sees trees, which turn out to be part of a low-lying island. He assumes the vision is a mirage, until he tests the island with his foot and smells the vegetation. The island is made largely of a kind of tubular seaweed, which Pi discovers is edible, and even delicious. He eats his fill and explores the island as much as he can (he is too weak to walk), but eventually Richard Parker ventures onto the island too, prompting Pi to return to the lifeboat to sleep, in case the new surroundings make Richard Parker dangerous again.

After two days Pi regains the ability to walk. Once he is strong enough to explore beyond the edges of the island, he finds that it is full of meerkats. It is also covered with ponds that Pi discovers to be freshwater, and from which the meerkats pull dead fish. It occurs to Pi that the algae somehow desalinates the water. Pi baths himself and cleans out the lifeboat using the fresh water.

Pi finds that the island possesses nothing but algae, trees, and meerkats; no other life whatsoever. Both Pi and Richard Parker manage to revive themselves, Pi with the algae, Richard Parker with the meerkats, and both with the fresh water and exercise. Richard Parker starts to get more aggressive, so Pi goes back to training him.

One night Pi finally decides to sleep out of the boat, and with his net makes a bed in one of the trees. While there, he sees all the meerkets suddenly desert their ponds and run to the forest, and all climb up into the trees. Pi enjoys sleeping with the meerkats, so he continues to do so, until the day he finds a tree at the center of the forest that appears to be the only tree to have fruit. When he tries to eat the fruit, he finds that each piece of fruit is actually layers and layers of leaves wrapped tightly around a human tooth; what's more, together the fruit form a full, perfect set of teeth. Pi's curiosity gets the best of him, and he tries to plant his feet on the island by night. The soil burns him terribly, however. It turns out that the island is carnivorous: it emits acid at night that dissolves anything on its surface. Pi must leave his semi-paradise, and is utterly weary as a result. He turns wholly to God.

Some time later, Pi and Richard Parker come upon land in what turns out to be Mexico. Richard Parker goes immediately off into the jungle without any kind of goodbye or acknowledgment to Pi. Soon Pi is found by humans, but he weeps over Richard Parker's desertion. The people who find him bathe him and feed him, and he is taken off to a hospital. He proclaims that this is the end of his story.

Analysis

This section continues the pattern created in the previous one, of great hopes followed by great disillusionment. When Pi discovers his island, it seems too good to be true—it has plenty of food, fresh water, meerkats for companionship, and protection from the weather. It is even moving, so there exists the potential that Pi could meet a ship, or other, human-inhabited land. Pi regains his strength, and some degree of happiness.

Yet while Pi seems to believe this island is a paradise, Martel's (and Pi the storyteller's) significant use of foreshadowing prevents the reader from ever truly believing it. Richard Parker's sore paws and refusal to stay on the island at night, the meerkats' panicked run to the trees, the disappearing fish, all foretell that something sinister is afoot. Pi does not give up his belief that this island is his perfect new home until he physically encounters the truth.

Pi the storyteller transitions abruptly from this realization to his coming upon land in Mexico. What happens in between - Pi's utter loss of all hope, his final turn to God - is told to us in one brief sentence. That is all. How and when Pi comes upon land is left unsaid; this again emphasizes the depth of Pi's loss of hope after learning the truth about the island. Pi, who normally cannot say enough about God and the rituals he uses to worship him, here says only that he turned fully to him.

This section also marks the betrayal by Richard Parker, a betrayal Pi can never forgive—not the killing of the Frenchman, but the act of leaving Pi without any indication of a goodbye. The resulting feeling of loss and sadness, rather than any excitement or relief at having finally returned to land, is what Pi emphasizes at the end of his story. The reader is thereby reminded that, although Pi has survived, he has lost all his family and everything he cared about, and now must face that loss within the human world.

Pi's declaration that this is the end of his story is also significant. Much in fact happens after his recuperation in Mexico. Positing "the end" when he does is a *choice*; the author, after all, does not end the story there, but instead includes an additional five chapters. Storytelling thus implies the ability to *choose* one's own story.

Summary and Analysis of Part 3

Summary

The author explains that what follows are transcripts of a recorded conversation between Pi and two men, Mr. Okamoto and Mr. Chiba, of the Maritime Department in the Japanese Ministry of Transport, after they come to see him in the hospital in Tomatlan, Mexico.

Mr. Okamoto gives Pi a cookie, and asks if he would be willing to tell them everything that happened to him. Chapter 97 says simply, "The story." After the story Mr. Okamoto and Mr. Chiba think Pi is fooling with them. They take a break, and Pi asks for another cookie.

Mr. Okamoto tells Pi that they don't believe his story because bananas don't float. Pi says that they do, and insists that they test it. They do, and it becomes clear that bananas do float. They tell Pi that they also don't believe him about the island, or about Richard Parker. Pi tries to convince them, and they remain hard to persuade. They insist that they want the true story, which leads Pi to tell them a completely different story.

In this new story, Pi (Richard Parker) ended up in the lifeboat with his mother (the orangutan), the cook (the hyena), and a sailor (the zebra). The cook was voracious, and ate things like flies and rats even when he still had plenty of rations left. The sailor was young, and had broken his leg getting into the lifeboat. He only knew Chinese, and he suffered greatly.

As the sailor's leg got infected, the cook said they must amputate it to save the sailor's life. This they did, using only surprise as an anesthetic. The cook later let it slip that he had amputated the leg to use it as fishing bait, but it was too decayed and did not work effectively. The sailor died, and the cook butchered him. He claimed this too was for bait, but after a few days he started eating the flesh himself. Pi and his mother never ate any of it, but they did start to eat the fish and the turtles that the cook captured from the sea.

One day Pi was too weak to pull in a turtle, and the cook hit him. His mother hit the cook back, and sent Pi to the raft. The cook killed the mother.

Eventually Pi got back onto the boat with the cook. They shared a turtle, then Pi killed the cook with the knife the cook left out. Pi subsequently ate some of the cook's organs and flesh.

Mr. Okamoto and Mr. Chiba notice the parallels in the two stories. They continue to question Pi about how the boat actually sank.

The final chapter contains Mr. Okamoto's report after the interrogation, in which he says that the cause of the *Tsimtsum*'s sinking is impossible to determine, and references Pi's amazing feat of having survived 227 days at sea with an adult tiger.

Analysis

Part 3 of *Life of Pi* revisits and reemphasizes themes raised earlier in the novel, as well as complicating and redefining them and the story itself. With the exceptions of the author's chapters scattered throughout the novel, Part 3 is the first significant portion of the text that departs from Pi's point of view to tell his story. This is especially significant, because Pi has claimed that his story is over; the author's choice to continue it is in a way a departure from Pi's presentation of, and thus control of, his story.

This idea of narrative *control* is crucial. Pi tells Mr. Okamoto and Mr. Chiba that everything in life is inherently a story - even facts, because they are being perceived by someone, and thus can never be truly objective. Yet in the mens' unwillingness to believe Pi's story, they weaken his control over it. Even faced with evidence—the floating bananas, the meerkat bones—they stand firm in their disbelief.

In response, Pi tells another story, one which should be more believable to them. In being forced to do so, he is in essence losing his control as storyteller - for the mens' dislike of zoo animals being involved must define how he tells the story.

Pi's second story is, seemingly, more realistic, as well as significantly more tragic and horrifying. In both stories, he survives a long and terrible ordeal, but in the second, he seems to contains both his own, rational self, and the ferocious, wild, and very dangerous Richard Parker. Even if this is not the "true" story, the possibility of such a division of Pi's personality is made clear by his doing so here—throughout his ordeal, we see his need to survive slowly overpowering his rational (vegetarian) self.

Yet while the second telling of the story may cast doubt for the reader on the first story, it is not meant to do so for more than a moment. Even the highly skeptical Mr. Okamoto and Mr. Chiba in the end choose to believe the first - the better story - because Pi tells them that they may. Neither story affects their investigation, so there is no reason not to take the less tragic and more "enjoyable" story as the true story. And this is how Pi finally defines his belief in God, and why Mr. Adirubasamy tells the author that this story will make him believe in God. Why not believe in a fundamentally benevolent universe?

Suggested Essay Questions

1. **Pi argues that Mr. Okamoto and Mr. Chiba should take the "better story" as the true story. Argue that either the first or second story is the "true story."**

   Suggested Answer: Either side can be argued. To argue that the first story is the true story: all characters in the text, even those originally skeptical, and including the author, eventually choose to believe the first story. Pi was greatly experienced with zoo animals, and manages to plausibly explain how he survived with Richard Parker for so long. Similarly, he seems truly depressed about Richard Parker's desertion, such that it is clear that he, at least, believes his second story. To argue that the second story is the true story: Pi's main argument to convince the skeptical Mr. Okamoto and Mr. Chiba that the first is true is that it is better, which is irrelevant in an argument about absolute truth.
2. **Yann Martel has said that the hyena is meant to represent cowardice. Explain how this is true.**

   Suggested Answer: The hyena displays many negative qualities, such as greed, stupidity and viciousness, but these qualities can be seen to come from its cowardice. At the beginning of their time in the boat, the hyena whines almost constantly, and is so afraid that it runs in circles until it makes itself sick. Unlike Pi, who even in his desperate fear finds ways to survive, the hyena just kills and eats as much as it can in a panicked state until Richard Parker kills it.
3. **In what ways does Pi parallel religious belief in God to the zoo?**

   Suggested Answer: The main parallel that Pi draws between these two things is the true freedom that both provide, even in seeming to restrict it. He says that detractors argue that zoos restrict animals' freedom and so make them unhappy, and the rituals and rules of religion can similarly be said to restrict human freedom. Pi argues, however, that zoos, by providing an animal with its survival needs, in fact give that animal as much freedom, for it is content, safe, and wouldn't want to leave. Similarly, the rules and ritual of religion in fact give people what Pi sees as their spiritual essentials, and thus a more significant kind of freedom.
4. **Yann Martel has called chapters 21 and 22 essential to the book. Why would this be so?**

   Suggested Anwer: These chapters deal explicitly with the promise of Pi's story's power given by Mr. Adirubasamy—that it will make the author, and by extension, the reader, believe in God. In chapter 21, that the author has begun to believe is very clear, and chapter 22 underscores Pi's belief in every atheist's potential to become a believer. The chapters together also underscore the act of storytelling, which Pi himself relates to a belief in God, by showing the author writing down the words which he then presents to us as Pi's own—and which are echoed at the end of the story, when Pi convinces Mr. Okamoto to believe in his story, and thus God.

5. **Both worship of God and survival are hugely important to Pi—which does he give primacy to?**

   Suggested Answer: Although Pi claims to have never lost faith in God, this faith clearly becomes less important to him while he is in his desperate fight to survive. Most obviously, he talks about God and his belief much less than in the chapters that deal with his life before and after his ordeal. He becomes to weak to perform his religious rituals with any regularity, but even more, he allows his need to survive to overpower his moral system. That is, he eats meat, kills living animals, and even goes so far as to eat human flesh.
6. **What are the significance of the stories behind how Pi and Richard Parker got their names?**

   Suggested Answer: Both Pi and Richard Parker's naming stories are related to water—Pi is named for a swimming pool, and Richard Parker's name was supposed to be Thirsty, because he drank so emphatically. Pi's water-related name is significant because he is the only member of his family who Mr. Adirubasamy can teach to swim, and although it does not explicitly save him, this ability gives Pi options while he is at sea. That Richard Parker ends up named after a man, rather than Thirsty as he is meant to be, is also significant because although Pi knows the danger of it, he eventually anthropomorphizes Richard Parker and so feels betrayed by him.
7. **Belief is a major theme in this novel. How are belief in God and belief in a story paralleled in *Life of Pi*?**

   Suggested Answer: Pi parallels the belief in God with the belief in a story by saying that everything in life is a story, because it is seen through a certain perspective, and thus altered by that perspective. If this is the case, he claims that something that doesn't change factual existence and cannot be determined finally either way can be chosen. Given this, one can, and should, choose the better story, which Pi believes is the story—the life—that includes a belief in God.
8. **Why is it significant that Pi is blind when he meets the Frenchman?**

   Suggested Answer: Pi's blindness is symbolic in many ways in the episode with the Frenchman. At the end of *Life of Pi*, Pi tells the Japanese officials that they would believe in the man-eating island if they had seen it, and thus ties belief to sight. Without sight, belief is much more difficult—so much so that Pi assumes he is hallucinating for much of his conversation with the Frenchman. But in the end he is able to believe without sight, an imperative for belief in God. His blindness is also significant because it parallels the literal darkness to the figurative darkness of the scene, which is perhaps the most disturbing of all of Pi's ordeal.

9. **Why does Pi give Richard Parker credit for his survival?**

   Suggested Answer: Richard Parker provides Pi with two things that are essential to his survival—companionship, and a surmountable obstacle. Although Richard Parker's presence at first seems like a death sentence, the challenges presented by it are in fact surmountable, as opposed to the loss of his family and the despair that it causes, which Pi can do nothing to alleviate. And although Richard Parker is dangerous, once Pi has tamed him, he does, in the wide open sea, provide a certain kind of companionship, which is deeply important to the utterly alone Pi.

10. **If each character in Pi's two stories are paralleled, Orange Juice to Pi's mother, the hyena to the cook, the sailor to the zebra, and Pi to Richard Parker, what does the Pi in the first story represent?**

    Suggested Answer: While Richard Parker in the first story is paralleled to Pi, it can be said that he is paralleled to Pi's survival instinct, while the Pi in the first story represents Pi's spirituality and morality. In this way, Pi's spirituality is able, with much hard work, to exert some control over his survival instinct—at least enough to remain in existence, even when not in control—while the survival instinct remains powerful and dangerous. Pi says that he would not have survived without Richard Parker, and this too is true in the parallel, for Pi's spirituality and morality needed Pi's survival instinct to keep his body alive, so that his spirituality could exist as well.

Survival at Sea

As is clear in *Life of Pi*, surviving for long periods of time at sea is extremely difficult, even without an adult tiger in the mix. Many experts consider survival at sea to be the most difficult survival situation. The three essentials of survival are protection from the elements, food, and water. Pi makes it clear that lack of abundant fresh water was his greatest stress at all times, and this is realistic: Pi was in a fairly hospitable climate and so faced little danger of freezing to death, and humans will die of dehydration long before they die from starvation. In fact, dehydration is such a danger that in a situation without abundant fresh water, survival experts recommend eating nothing rather than eating protein, which requires water from the body's store to be digested.

In situations like Pi's, where there is limited protection from the sun, experts recommend wetting skin and clothes with salt water, which helps prevent loss of body water through sweating. They also recommend being as still as possible during the heat of the day, and doing essential activities at dawn and dusk to minimize sweating. Although Pi finds that his seasickness is never as severe as Orange Juice's or Richard Parker's, seasickness can be dangerous in trying to survive at sea, for the vomiting it can cause will further dehydration and weakening.

Pi is also correct not to try to survive in the water in order to distance himself from Richard Parker—life expectancy in a survival at sea situation is much worse for those who do not have a boat or raft. Even in the warmest waters, life expectancy is only twelve hours, and it quickly drops the colder the water is.

Drinking seawater and urine are both, Pi is correct to believe, dangerous, and hurry the process of death by dehydration. Even drinking seawater diluted with fresh water is dangerous and not helpful. Pi is also correct that turtle blood is a safe method of hydration, and there is also potable liquid in fish eyes and fish spinal fluid. Although some fish can be poisonous, generally fish that are available when you cannot see land are safe. Solar stills are known to be theoretically helpful, but often do not work well in practice.

The side-effects of dehydration can include headache, irritability, dizziness, faintness, rapid pulse, shallow breathing, pins and needles, and after that, hallucinations and delirium, preceding death. Blindness, however, is not a common side-effect.

Author of ClassicNote and Sources

Alice Cullina, author of ClassicNote. Completed on November 03, 2008, copyright held by GradeSaver.

Updated and revised Damien Chazelle November 30, 2008. Copyright held by GradeSaver.

Painter, Corinne and Christian Lotz, eds.. Phenomenology and the Non-Human Animal: At the Limits of Experience . Dordrecht, The Netherlands: Springer, 2007.

Golden, Frank and Michael Tipton. Essentials of Survival at Sea. Champaign, Illinois: Human Kinetics, 2002.

Martel, Yann. "How I Wrote Life of Pi." 2008-10-17. <http://www.powells.com/fromtheauthor/martel.html>.

"Yann Martel." Gale Literary Databases, Contemporary Literary Criticism. 2008-10-18. <http://galenet.galegroup.com>.

"Yann Martel." Literature Online biography. 2008-10-20. <http://lion.chadwyck.com>.

"The Open Sea." Wilderness Survival. 2008-10-28. <http://www.wilderness-survival.net/sea-1.php>.

Mishra, Pankaj. "The Man, or the Tiger?" *New York Reveiw of Books* 50, no. 5. 27 March 2003: 17-18.

Essay: Living a Lie: Yann Martel's Pi and his Dissociation from Reality

by Sean Patrick Ewart
November 19, 2008

Piscine Molitor Patel, the protagonist of Yann Martel's acclaimed novel Life of Pi, survives a horrific 227-day ordeal trapped aboard a directionless lifeboat with only a 450-pound Bengal Tiger, named Richard Parker, for company. Pi's account of his misfortune spans the majority of the work, and it takes him hours to recount it to the Japanese investigators at the novel's conclusion. His description is so vivid, so extensive, and so detailed that it would seem, despite its admittedly outlandish elements, deeply founded in actual events. Indeed, to fabricate something of such intensity would be unthinkable—and this is in fact the case. Pi almost unthinkingly constructs a fantasy alternative to the appalling truth of his experience in order to shield his psyche from the truly dreadful circumstances of his survival. Pi alters the actuality of his time on the lifeboat in such an unwitting manner as to be able to believe this figment of his imagination without hesitation, insistent on the truthfulness of his original account. It is only after a "Long silence" that Pi is able to bear witness to the actual facts regarding his experiences on the lifeboat (381). Author Joan Didion suggests that we must "tell ourselves stories in order to live." This statement bears a special significance to Pi's situation on the lifeboat, and his subsequent subconscious confusion between the story of cannibalism, butchery and murder that rang true, and his more pleasing, fantastical construct in which all of the negative elements of the true account are projected onto a tactless wild animal. Didion would argue that this "story", including the array of wild animals accompanying Pi on his drift across the Pacific, is merely the one he tells himself in order to live, and in order to protect himself from going entirely mad.

Pi's survival on the lifeboat, beginning July 2nd 1977 and not ending for some 227 days, continues due only to the absolute ruthlessness with which his fellow survivor, the Frenchman, conducts himself. In addition to the Frenchman, Pi's mother and a badly injured Chinese sailor are also aboard the lifeboat at first (382). Immediately identifying the sailor as a weakness, the Frenchman quickly maneuvers Pi and his mother into "helping" the sailor by aiding the Frenchman in amputating the sailor's leg (383). Immediately after this, however, we learn the Frenchman has done so only in order to secure bait for his fishing lines (384). Over the course of the ordeal, Pi witnesses increasingly horrid acts of inhumanity, all in the name of survival: the Frenchman promptly butchers the sailor's body once he dies, including "pull[ing] off his face" (387). When fishing proves not immediately successful, the Frenchman begins to eat the sailor's corpse: "'Tastes like pork,' he muttered" (388). As the situation onboard deteriorates, the cook resorts to murder to feed himself:

"They were fighting. I did nothing but watch. My mother was fighting an adult man. He was mean and muscular. He caught her by the wrist and twisted it. She shrieked and fell. He moved over her. The knife appeared. He raised it in the air. It came down. Next it was up—it was red. It went up and down repeatedly. I couldn't see her. She was at the bottom of the boat. I saw only him. He stopped. He raised his head and looked at me. He hurled something my way. A line of blood struck me across the face. No whip could have inflicted a more painful lash. I held my mother's head in my hands... He appeared when he threw my mother's body overboard. His mouth was red." (389-390)

The cook's depravity and the unimaginably macabre concept of holding one's own mother's decapitated head would doubtless have far-reaching effects on a developing child's mental state. As scarring as that could be, however, it could only be compounded by subsequent murder and cannibalism—"I stabbed him in the throat, next to the Adam's apple. He dropped like a stone... His heart was a struggle—all those tubes that connected it. I managed to get it out. It tasted delicious" (391). This cataclysm of psychologically devastating occurrences would no doubt cause irreversible damage to anyone forced to face them without some sort of coping mechanism. Pi, as we see, develops a very effective mechanism of his own.

"We interpret what we see, select the most workable of the multiple choices" states Didion. This is directly applicable to Pi's situation. He sees, of course, the grisly events on the lifeboat committed not only by the Frenchman, but also by himself. Despite this seemingly immovable pillar of fact, Pi "interprets" what he sees into a more palatable form, one that gilds over the scenes of desperation and human depravity he witnesses. He refuses to accept the actual circumstances of his survival, and instead fabricates an alternate reality he steps into whenever the truth becomes too unbearable. He replaces the people around him with things familiar to him; in his case, these are wild animals from his father's zoo in India. The similarities between the two stories Pi tells have inescapable parallels: with himself playing the role of Richard Parker, a crippled zebra in place of the Chinese sailor with the broken leg, Orange Juice the orangutan in place of his mother, and the French cook doing double duty as both the hyena and himself. Pi relays his fantasy with such striking imagery and unhesitating confidence that it seems entirely plausible: the wicked cook cuts off the sailor's leg, using it as fishing bait, but later consumes the entire sailor, much as the hyena did with the crippled zebra. Later, the Frenchman also kills Pi's mother, just as the hyena killed Orange Juice. In the end, Pi ends up killing the Frenchman, just as Richard Parker had dispatched both the hyena and the Frenchman. These parallels between the two stories are very apparent, and this fact brings additional credence to Didion's statement. Pi "select[s] the most workable of the multiple choices" of stories, preferring the one which he creates for himself as a safe haven against the mental torment of the human depredation around him. This subconscious disconnect from reality is likely what preserved Pi's sanity, or at least some of it, during the tumultuous 227 days he was at sea. By choosing the "most workable choice," Pi manages to survive his ordeal with his psyche intact.

Indeed, Joan Didion's assertion that we must "tell ourselves stories in order to live" is perfectly demonstrated by the protagonist in Yann Martel's Life of Pi. Without existing within a wholly fabricated story of his own creation, Pi Patel could have in no way survived the immense mental and physical hardships that beset him at sea. Either from madness or by suicide, Pi would have certainly perished had he been forced to accept the events that occurred at face value. The unbelievably tortuous experiences of watching a man be butchered for fishing bait, of watching one's mother murdered, decapitated, and feasted upon, of oneself committing murder, would be impossible to overcome without some sort of psychological aid; Pi's fanciful story of orangutans, carnivorous islands, and Bengal tigers become this aid. It acts as a sort of security blanket, something to retreat into when difficulty arises. The fact that it takes Pi some time to recall the actual events onboard the lifeboat point to how thoroughly he has espoused this construct of his. To have retreated so fully into his world of fantasy, Pi must certainly have subconsciously recognized the danger to his psychological state that such grisly occurrences posed. He truly had to tell himself this "story" in order to live.

Quiz 1

1. **Who has the worst sea sickness?**
    A. Richard Parker
    B. Pi
    C. Ravi
    D. Orange Juice

2. **Where does Pi grow up?**
    A. Munnar
    B. Zurich
    C. Toronto
    D. Pondicherry

3. **How does Richard Parker get his name?**
    A. He resembles a famous actor named Richard Parker.
    B. Pi names him after favorite teacher.
    C. A clerical error
    D. His zookeeper names him after himself.

4. **What does Pi use as the base of his raft?**
    A. The tarpaulin
    B. The zebra's bones
    C. Oars
    D. Planks from the boat

5. **What does Pi consider to be his saving grace after the big storm?**
    A. That Richard Parker was subdued by the storm
    B. That the food stores survived
    C. That one whistle is not lost, so he can still control Richard Parker
    D. That the raft is undamaged

6. **What is Pi's first religion?**
    A. Christianity
    B. Buddhism
    C. Hinduism
    D. Islam

7. **What did Pi forget that made his ordeal easier?**
   A. His past
   B. His family
   C. Time
   D. His religion

8. **What bait does Pi use to fish the first time?**
   A. Biscuits
   B. His leather shoe
   C. Scraps from the hyena's carcass
   D. Bits of chocolate

9. **What was Pi grateful to Richard Parker for?**
   A. He killed the dangerous hyena.
   B. He distracted him from the despair of being utterly alone and having lost his family.
   C. He provided warmth.
   D. His weight kept the boat steadier.

10. **What does Pi have a hard time bringing himself to do?**
   A. Put the zebra out of its misery after the hyena tears its leg off
   B. Kill the first dorado he catches
   C. Eat the zebra once it's been killed
   D. Kill the flying fish to use as bait

11. **What punishment does Pi use to tame Richard Parker?**
   A. Pulling his tail
   B. A shrill whistle
   C. Splashing him with water
   D. Seasickness

12. **What does Pi's period of blindness represent to him?**
   A. The beginning of his real moral suffering
   B. His profound faith
   C. His loneliest time
   D. His profound ability to survive

13. **What does Pi use to enter a dream-like state?**
    A. Slightly rotten fish
    B. Richard Parker's urine
    C. Semi-starvation
    D. A damp cloth

14. **What does Pi say is life's only true opponent?**
    A. Despair
    B. Fear
    C. Lack of faith in God
    D. Death

15. **What is Pi's real name?**
    A. Piscine
    B. Pi
    C. Pondicherry
    D. P. Singh

16. **What aspect of Pi's personality makes his survival struggle even harder?**
    A. His sensitivity to sunlight
    B. His vegetarianism
    C. His allergy to cats
    D. His fear of the ocean

17. **In Pi's second story, who or what is the cook paralleled to?**
    A. Richard Parker
    B. The zebra
    C. The hyena
    D. Pi's survival instinct

18. **Which of these is not part of Pi's taming of Richard Parker?**
    A. Holding and smelling Richard Parker's feces
    B. Making Richard Parker seasick
    C. Stealing Richard Parker's food
    D. Blowing a whistle aggressively

19. **What is Pi's reaction the first time that he sees a faucet gushing water after his ordeal?**
   A. He drinks for ten minutes straight
   B. He faints
   C. He drops to his knees and prays
   D. He collects the water in every container he has and stores it

20. **What causes the author discomfort when he visits Pi?**
   A. The religious symbols all over Pi's house
   B. The weird silence in the house, even when all of Pi's family is home
   C. The spiciness of the food that Pi always serves him
   D. Pi's cat, to whom the author is allergic

21. **What animal does Pi choose for the topic of his zoology thesis?**
   A. Meerkat
   B. Laughing hyena
   C. Three-toed sloth
   D. Bengal tiger

22. **When Pi goes blind, what starts to bring his vision back?**
   A. The first food he eats
   B. It comes back spontaneously
   C. His tears
   D. The sea turtle's blood he drinks

23. **What does Pi say is the only body part that functions well while one is undergoing fear?**
   A. The ears
   B. The eyes
   C. The heart
   D. The lungs

24. **What does Pi consider his best plan to get rid of Richard Parker?**
   A. Kill him with morphine
   B. Strangle him with rope
   C. Survive until he dies of starvation or thirst
   D. Push him off the boat

25. **What is commonly referred to as the most dangerous animal in a zoo?**

A. The polar bear
B. The tiger
C. Man
D. The gorilla

Quiz 1 Answer Key

1. **(D)** Orange Juice
2. **(D)** Pondicherry
3. **(C)** A clerical error
4. **(C)** Oars
5. **(C)** That one whistle is not lost, so he can still control Richard Parker
6. **(C)** Hinduism
7. **(C)** Time
8. **(B)** His leather shoe
9. **(B)** He distracted him from the despair of being utterly alone and having lost his family.
10. **(D)** Kill the flying fish to use as bait
11. **(D)** Seasickness
12. **(A)** The beginning of his real moral suffering
13. **(D)** A damp cloth
14. **(B)** Fear
15. **(A)** Piscine
16. **(B)** His vegetarianism
17. **(C)** The hyena
18. **(C)** Stealing Richard Parker's food
19. **(B)** He faints
20. **(C)** The spiciness of the food that Pi always serves him
21. **(C)** Three-toed sloth
22. **(C)** His tears
23. **(B)** The eyes
24. **(C)** Survive until he dies of starvation or thirst
25. **(C)** Man

Quiz 2

1. **What does Pi offer to the Japanese men as evidence of his story?**
   A. The simple fact of his own survival
   B. The presence of tiger excrement in the boat
   C. The claw marks from Richard Parker all over the boat
   D. The presence of meerkat bones in the boat

2. **What is the story that Pi tells the Frenchman about?**
   A. A banana
   B. His family
   C. A tiger and a hyena
   D. Jesus and Muhammad

3. **What offering does Pi give Richard Parker as he comes onto the tarpaulin?**
   A. The zebra's leg
   B. The hyena
   C. A rat
   D. Part of the chocolate bar

4. **What desire of Pi's causes his parents distress?**
   A. To be on the swim team
   B. To feed the tigers at the zoo
   C. To go to Catholic school
   D. To get a prayer rug and be baptized

5. **What does Pi say was his greatest wish other than salvation?**
   A. To have paper and a writing utensil
   B. To have Indian food
   C. To have a book
   D. To get rid of Richard Parker

6. **What does Pi say brought him back to life after his suffering?**
   A. Academic study and religion
   B. Meeting his wife
   C. His foster family's care and love
   D. The challenge of adjusting to his new country

7. **What eventually stops Pi from writing in his diary?**
    A. His pen runs out of ink
    B. He loses all hope
    C. He becomes too weak
    D. He runs out of paper

8. **What leads Pi to realize he should tame Richard Parker instead of trying to get rid of him?**
    A. Richard Parker protects Pi from the sharks
    B. Richard Parker backs off when Pi throws him the rat
    C. Pi almost drowns in a storm because he is stuck on the raft
    D. Richard Parker makes the prusten call

9. **Why does Pi think the Frenchman he meets while blind is Richard Parker?**
    A. Because the Frenchman tells Pi that he is the tiger
    B. Because Richard Parker came from a French zoo
    C. Because he can't imagine there is anyone else nearby
    D. Because he seems to be very carnivorous

10. **Right after the Tsimtsum sinks, why does Pi jump out of the lifeboat?**
    A. He realizes he has just encouraged a tiger onto the boat
    B. To grab a bunch of bananas
    C. He wants to return to his family
    D. To try to save Orange Juice

11. **What is Ravi especially interested in?**
    A. Sports
    B. Religions
    C. Predators
    D. Boats

12. **Which of these is a primary theme of Life of Pi?**
    A. Overcoming loss
    B. The connection between stories and reality
    C. Cultural identity
    D. Coming of age

13. **Who does Pi worry he will not be able to recognize?**
    A. Father Martin
    B. Mr. Kumar the baker
    C. Himself, after his ordeal
    D. Mr. Kumar the teacher

14. **Which of these factors leads Pi to realize he cannot win a war of attrition against Richard Parker?**
    A. Bengal tigers can drink certain levels of saline water
    B. Richard Parker plunders Pi's food supplies
    C. Richard Parker learns to fish
    D. Pi runs out of fresh water

15. **According to Pi, when will any large cat not attack?**
    A. When it is not hungry
    B. While the prey's back is turned
    C. While the prey is making direct eye contract with it
    D. While a more alpha cat is present

16. **What did Pi do with the cigarettes he had?**
    A. Ate them
    B. Traded them for a space on the lifeboat
    C. Fed them to Richard Parker
    D. Used them to create smoke signals

17. **Which of these did not help save Pi's life?**
    A. Richard Parker
    B. His raft
    C. The flares
    D. His whistles

18. **What does Pi like to look at in the water?**
    A. The sky's reflection
    B. His reflection
    C. The undersea communities
    D. Signs of nearby land

19. **What is finally determined as the cause of the Tsimtsum sinking?**
   A. It is never determined.
   B. It collided with another ship.
   C. An explosion below deck
   D. Damage from a storm

20. **Which character introduces the author to Pi's story?**
   A. Francis Adirubasamy
   B. Tomohiro Okamoto
   C. Meena Patel
   D. Asuro Chiba

21. **What does Pi's father love to talk about, although he has no firsthand knowledge of it?**
   A. Hunting
   B. Swimming
   C. Tigers in the wild
   D. Canada

22. **What two things does Pi argue have more in common than one would expect?**
   A. Tigers and man
   B. Zoology and religion
   C. India and Canada
   D. Survival and literature

23. **What does Pi consider very dangerous when dealing with animals?**
   A. The assumption that you are smarter than they are
   B. Finding them cute or beautiful
   C. The tendency to show fear
   D. The tendency to anthropomorphize them

24. **Which of these adjectives best describes Pi?**
   A. Cynical
   B. Passive
   C. Precocious
   D. Consistent

25. **What makes a Canadian waiter accuse Pi of being "fresh off the boat?"**

A. He eats with his fingers.

B. He has trouble with the Canadian money.

C. His strong accent

D. He complains that the food is not as it would be in India

Quiz 2 Answer Key

1. **(D)** The presence of meerkat bones in the boat
2. **(A)** A banana
3. **(C)** A rat
4. **(D)** To get a prayer rug and be baptized
5. **(C)** To have a book
6. **(A)** Academic study and religion
7. **(A)** His pen runs out of ink
8. **(D)** Richard Parker makes the prusten call
9. **(D)** Because he seems to be very carnivorous
10. **(A)** He realizes he has just encouraged a tiger onto the boat
11. **(A)** Sports
12. **(B)** The connection between stories and reality
13. **(B)** Mr. Kumar the baker
14. **(A)** Bengal tigers can drink certain levels of saline water
15. **(C)** While the prey is making direct eye contract with it
16. **(A)** Ate them
17. **(C)** The flares
18. **(C)** The undersea communities
19. **(A)** It is never determined.
20. **(A)** Francis Adirubasamy
21. **(B)** Swimming
22. **(B)** Zoology and religion
23. **(D)** The tendency to anthropomorphize them
24. **(C)** Precocious
25. **(A)** He eats with his fingers.

Quiz 3

1. **When they are on the island, why does Richard Parker always return to the boat at night?**
   A. To stash all of the meerkats he has hunted
   B. Because he wants to defend his territory
   C. Because he only feels safe in his territory
   D. Because the island's surface becomes acidic

2. **What is plan number six for Pi's survival?**
   A. Swim to safety
   B. Build a life raft
   C. Let Richard Parker kill the hyena, then push him off the boat
   D. Wage a war of attrition against Richard Parker

3. **What does Pi dislike about agnostics?**
   A. That they do not respect religion
   B. That they do not believe in God
   C. That they don't search for truth
   D. That they do not have faith either way, but only doubt

4. **Why does Pi choose the sloth for his thesis?**
   A. He saw it as the opposite of the tiger.
   B. His father always told him it was the most fascinating animal to study.
   C. Its calm demeanor and slowness soothes him.
   D. It had been his favorite animal at the Pondicherry Zoo.

5. **What does Richard Parker do that Pi cannot get over?**
   A. Kills the orangutan
   B. Leaves him without saying goodbye
   C. Steals all of Pi's food whenever he can
   D. Tries to kill him after they have learned to live together

6. **What causes Pi to imagine his father feeding him to his lions?**
   A. Nightmares after his father shows him the tiger killing a goat
   B. His feeling of betrayal at having to leave Pondicherry for Canada
   C. An attempt to understand Jesus's death as atonement for man's sins
   D. His feeling of betrayal at his father not understanding his religious desires

7. **What does Pi study at the University of Toronto?**
   A. Religion and zoology
   B. Animal psychology and engineering
   C. Literature and marine biology
   D. Religion and literature

8. **Ravi's threat that Pi is "the next goat" is an example of what literary technique?**
   A. Simile
   B. Foreshadowing
   C. Allegory
   D. Personification

9. **Which of these statements is incorrect?**
   A. The cook and the hyena are parallel figures.
   B. Richard Parker can be seen as a symbol for Pi's survival instinct.
   C. Richard Parker is the antagonist of Life of Pi.
   D. Pi Patel is the protagonist of Life of Pi.

10. **Which of the following first disturbs Pi about Christianity?**
   A. Christianity's lack of tolerance for Hindus
   B. The history of violence in the name of Christianity
   C. The Catholic reliance on ritual
   D. That a god would be willing to suffer humiliation and death

11. **Who is Santosh?**
   A. Pi's son
   B. Pi's favorite teacher
   C. Pi's father
   D. Pi's brother

12. **Which quote epitomizes a central theme of Life of Pi?**
   A. "Yet there will always be animals that seek to escape from zoos."
   B. "I picked up the knife and fork. I had hardly ever used such instruments. My hands trembled. My sambar lost its taste."
   C. "I had no idea a living being could sustain so much injury and go on living."
   D. "Which is the better story?"

13. **What causes something inside Pi to die?**
    A. Becoming too weak to perform his prayers
    B. Realizing that he lost his faith during his ordeal
    C. Having to eat meat
    D. Richard Parker saving Pi's life by killing another man

14. **What mistake does Richard Parker make?**
    A. He puts his paw into a shark's mouth.
    B. He jumps into the ocean while bloody.
    C. He sleeps on the carnivorous island.
    D. He eats the rotten hyena flesh which makes him sick.

15. **Which of these was not one of the great pleasures of the island to Pi?**
    A. The smell of the soil
    B. Having unlimited fresh water
    C. Being in the shade of a tree
    D. The sweetness of the algae

16. **Which of these themes is present primarily in the framing to the main story?**
    A. The significance of suffering
    B. The primacy of survival
    C. The connection between science and religion
    D. The relativity of freedom

17. **What does the most damage to Pi's skin?**
    A. The sun
    B. His allergy to Richard Parker
    C. Splinters from the boat
    D. Salt

18. **"Life will defend itself no matter how small it is. Every animal is ferocious and dangerous." Name the speaker**
    A. The Frenchman
    B. Pi
    C. Pi's father
    D. Pi's mother

19. **What does Pi's father do to make sure he acts safely around tigers?**
A. Tells Pi that God does not like him to be near tigers
B. Tells him that tigers' favorite food is little boys
C. Makes Pi always stand ten feet away from the tiger cage
D. Makes Pi watch while he puts a goat in a cage with a hungry tiger

20. **How does Pi believe the animals got out of their cages on the Tsimtsum?**
A. Their cages were opened in the explosion.
B. They were never properly restrained, and the flooding on the ship motivated their escape.
C. His father released them so they could save themselves as the ship went down.
D. A drunken member of the crew let them out.

21. **What does Pi think most people wrongly believe about animals?**
A. That they are afraid of people
B. That they enjoy hunting
C. That they act only by instinct or rote
D. That freedom means happiness for them

22. **What does Pi believe happens to an atheist upon his deathbed?**
A. He makes a leap of faith, and believes in God
B. He sees a light and assumes it is a failing of oxygen in his brain
C. He dies confident in his disbelief in God
D. He sees all of his mistakes

23. **What is Pi's brother's name?**
A. Satish
B. Santosh
C. Molitor
D. Ravi

24. **Who does Pi believe is beholden to "dry, yeastless factuality"?**
A. Atheists
B. Agnostics
C. Scientists
D. Theologians

25. **What does Pi's father consider himself to be?**

A. Modern
B. A true Indian patriot
C. A great swimmer
D. Pious

Quiz 3 Answer Key

1. **(D)** Because the island's surface becomes acidic
2. **(D)** Wage a war of attrition against Richard Parker
3. **(D)** That they do not have faith either way, but only doubt
4. **(C)** Its calm demeanor and slowness soothes him.
5. **(B)** Leaves him without saying goodbye
6. **(C)** An attempt to understand Jesus's death as atonement for man's sins
7. **(A)** Religion and zoology
8. **(B)** Foreshadowing
9. **(C)** Richard Parker is the antagonist of Life of Pi.
10. **(D)** That a god would be willing to suffer humiliation and death
11. **(C)** Pi's father
12. **(D)** "Which is the better story?"
13. **(D)** Richard Parker saving Pi's life by killing another man
14. **(A)** He puts his paw into a shark's mouth.
15. **(A)** The smell of the soil
16. **(C)** The connection between science and religion
17. **(D)** Salt
18. **(C)** Pi's father
19. **(D)** Makes Pi watch while he puts a goat in a cage with a hungry tiger
20. **(D)** A drunken member of the crew let them out.
21. **(D)** That freedom means happiness for them
22. **(A)** He makes a leap of faith, and believes in God
23. **(D)** Ravi
24. **(B)** Agnostics
25. **(A)** Modern

Quiz 4

1. **"There are no grounds for going beyond a scientific explanation of reality and no sound reason for believing anything but our sense experience." Name the speaker**
   A. Pi
   B. Mr. Okamoto
   C. Pi's father
   D. Mr. Kumar the teacher

2. **Which of these did not foreshadow the island's carnivorous nature?**
   A. The disappearance of the dead fish and shark
   B. The bad taste of the inside of the algae
   C. Richard Parker's sore paws
   D. That the meerkats all slept in the trees

3. **What strange objects did the Frenchman eat?**
   A. Pieces of wood from his boat
   B. Pieces of a lifejacket
   C. Cigarettes
   D. Boots

4. **Which of these afflictions does Pi never suffer from?**
   A. Constipation
   B. Deafness
   C. Blindness
   D. Boils

5. **What was "the terrible cost of Richard Parker"?**
   A. That Pi had to feed him the majority of their food
   B. That Pi had to be constantly afraid
   C. That he destroyed the fresh water stills
   D. That he killed the Frenchman

6. **Which surprising cross-species friendship exists at the Pondicherry Zoo?**
   A. A tiger and a dog
   B. A hippo and a lion
   C. A rhino and a herd of goats
   D. An elephant and three guinea pigs

7. **Why are animal enclosures cleaned carefully?**
   A. To show the animals that the zookeepers are in charge of their environment
   B. So the visitors aren't offended by the smell
   C. So the animals don't become depressed
   D. So the animals don't eat their parasite-infected feces

8. **Which of these convinces Pi that he has found land?**
   A. Testing it with his foot
   B. His sense of smell
   C. Seeing a bird
   D. Seeing trees

9. **Where is Pondicherry?**
   A. Mexico
   B. Sri Lanka
   C. South India
   D. Central India

10. **Which character does Pi describe as especially funny looking?**
   A. His father
   B. Mr. Kumar the baker
   C. Orange Juice
   D. Mr. Kumar the teacher

11. **Which of these was not a hurdle for Mr. Okamoto and Mr. Chiba getting to Pi?**
   A. Their difficulty speaking English
   B. A mechanic scammed them
   C. They went to the wrong town first
   D. Their car broke down

12. **Which of these does Pi never try to eat?**
   A. Richard Parker's feces
   B. A cigarette
   C. Human flesh
   D. A boot

13. **Which animal symbolizes maternity?**

A. Richard Parker

B. The zebra

C. Orange Juice

D. The meerkats

14. **Where does the author claim to have come upon Pi's story?**

A. Mexico

B. America

C. India

D. Canada

15. **Which of these facts surprises the author about Pi?**

A. That he is thin

B. That he has many religious icons in his house

C. That he has a family

D. That he is a good cook

16. **Why aren't animals in the wild truly free?**

A. Humans encroach on their habitats.

B. You can only be free if you can understand freedom.

C. They are restricted by their survival needs.

D. Their societies have very strict social rules.

17. **What does Pi wish he could be at one moment in the book?**

A. A tiger

B. The ocean

C. Lightning

D. A tree

18. **Who claims that Pi's story will "make you believe in God"?**

A. Francis Adirubasamy

B. Pi

C. Santosh Kumar the baker

D. The author

19. **Which of these does Pi use for protection while training Richard Parker?**
    A. The gaff
    B. Turtle shields
    C. An oar
    D. A life jacket

20. **Which of these is evidence of Pi's dominance over Richard Parker?**
    A. Richard Parker won't look Pi in the eye.
    B. Richard Parker won't eat until Pi is finished.
    C. Richard Parker tries to hide his feces.
    D. Richard Parker makes the prusten call.

21. **Which of these does Pi prove to be untrue?**
    A. That tigers hate water
    B. That bananas don't float
    C. That algae can't be carnivorous
    D. That orangutans are vegetarians

22. **What makes the author say that Pi's story has a happy ending?**
    A. Pi and Richard Parker both survive
    B. Pi finds out his mother survived, too
    C. Pi says that he became a better person because of his ordeal
    D. Meeting Pi's family

23. **Which of these is not a motif in Life of Pi?**
    A. Ritual
    B. Dominance
    C. Suffering
    D. Competition

24. **What does Pi abhor for life after his ordeal?**
    A. Cats
    B. Salt
    C. Cumin
    D. Water

25. **When does Pi return to Pondicherry?**

A. As soon as he has recovered from his ordeal

B. On his honeymoon

C. Never

D. After he graduates from University of Toronto

Quiz 4 Answer Key

1. **(D)** Mr. Kumar the teacher
2. **(B)** The bad taste of the inside of the algae
3. **(D)** Boots
4. **(B)** Deafness
5. **(D)** That he killed the Frenchman
6. **(C)** A rhino and a herd of goats
7. **(D)** So the animals don't eat their parasite-infected feces
8. **(B)** His sense of smell
9. **(C)** South India
10. **(D)** Mr. Kumar the teacher
11. **(A)** Their difficulty speaking English
12. **(D)** A boot
13. **(C)** Orange Juice
14. **(C)** India
15. **(C)** That he has a family
16. **(C)** They are restricted by their survival needs.
17. **(D)** A tree
18. **(A)** Francis Adirubasamy
19. **(B)** Turtle shields
20. **(C)** Richard Parker tries to hide his feces.
21. **(B)** That bananas don't float
22. **(D)** Meeting Pi's family
23. **(D)** Competition
24. **(B)** Salt
25. **(C)** Never

ClassicNotes

Getting you the grade since 1999™

Made in the USA
Middletown, DE
04 September 2015